# PRAISE FOR *A LETTER FOR EVERY MOTHER*

"Kara and Regan have managed to capture the entire essence of being a mother—the highs, the lows, and everything in between—in this beautiful collection of essays. You will find yourself comforted by the commonalities we all face, and reminded that, even though it doesn't always feel like it, we're all on the same side. Motherhood, like the words on these pages, unites us."

—Jill Smokler of *Scary Mommy*,
*New York Times* bestselling author

"While one of the most extraordinary experiences, motherhood can be one of the most isolating experiences a woman will ever face. All that most of us want to hear is that we are not alone on this crazy ride—and that is just what *A Letter for Every Mother* will accomplish. Compiling a collection of stories that every single person in this market will relate to, with a message that each of them craves, is a genius move. I believe this book will sell itself and I can't wait to see it published."

—Tori Grenz, editor of *Mamalode*

# A Letter for Every Mother

KARA LAWLER AND REGAN LONG

**CENTER STREET**

New York Nashville

Center Street
Hachette Book Group
1290 Avenue of the Americas, New York, NY 10104
centerstreet.com
twitter.com/centerstreet

First Hardcover Edition: April 2018

Center Street is a division of Hachette Book Group, Inc. The Center Street name and logo are trademarks of Hachette Book Group, Inc.

The publisher is not responsible for websites (or their content) that are not owned by the publisher.

The Hachette Speakers Bureau provides a wide range of authors for speaking events. To find out more, go to www.HachetteSpeakersBureau.com or call (866) 376-6591.

Library of Congress Cataloging-in-Publication Data has been applied for.

ISBNs: 978-1-4789-2243-8 (paper-over-board), 978-1-4789-2244-5 (ebook)

Printed in the United States of America

LSC-C

10 9 8 7 6 5 4 3 2 1

# Contents

## Contents

Contents

*For our children:*
*Matt and Maggie*
*Kendyl, Kaden, Kennedy, and Kelsey*

# *Foreword*

# BY ASHLEY WILLIS

*Motherhood.* Doesn't that word sound kind of funny? It sounds so sterile and formal, and yet, being a mom is anything but that. It's messy, crazy, exciting, wonderful, laughable, frustrating, tiring, and so much more all rolled into one. It's sticky hands, clogged toilets, dances in the rain, goose eggs on foreheads, and lots of tickles. It's bringing home a bad report card but making the winning touchdown on the same day. It's teenage angst mixed with heartfelt conversations over dinner. It's eating breakfast together and laughing until milk pours out your nostrils. It's your toddler spilling his drink for the 4,557th time. It's terrifying, magical, and magnificent. It's exhausting in the best way. It's an ongoing, work-in-progress kind of calling like nothing else on earth. That's real motherhood.

There are lots of us mommies out there, and yet we sometimes feel so alone in our mothering. Why is that? I think most of us are afraid. We're scared that we are the only ones whose kids aren't hitting the milestones. We hide our faces and cringe as our children seem to be the only kids who don't sit quietly in the shopping cart while we shop for groceries. We cry alone in our pantries and tell ourselves that we aren't cut out to be good moms, and then we dry our eyes and put on a smile for the friends coming over for dinner. When asked if we are okay, we'll say yes, but inside our hearts, we know that's not the truth and wonder if we're the only moms who are struggling.

Sweet Mama, you are not the only one. Every mom experiences struggles and triumphs. It's part of the beautiful calling of motherhood, and that is exactly why *A Letter for Every Mother* is a must-read. Both writers as well as mothers, Regan Long and Kara Lawler share their heartfelt thoughts and experiences through honest words and insightful perspective. In a collection of letters, Long and Lawler address motherhood and the various seasons we all go through as moms head-on.

With letters like "Dear Crying Baby," "Dear Friend: You Are Enough," and "To THAT Family," Long and Lawler magnificently weave humor and heart throughout their sincere and poignant testimonies to motherhood. They even address specific mom experiences in letters like "To the Mom of the Autistic Child." As seasoned bloggers who have written numerous viral posts for the *Huffington Post*, *Scary Mommy*, and other publications, Long and Lawler join forces to utilize their undoubted writing talent and their personal experiences of motherhood to encourage every mom, no matter the circumstance.

One of my favorite letters in the book is "To the Mom on the

Sidelines at the Water Park." This letter explores how one mom, Lawler, chooses to stay on the sidelines and refuses to put on a swimsuit because in her mind, her body isn't good enough. She's embarrassed, frustrated, and feels inadequate. As she is standing there watching her little one play in the splash area, another mother catches her eye. Lawler is struck by the sheer joy beaming from this mom's face as she splashes around—uninhibited by the swimsuit she wears on her unchiseled body—with her kids and others all around. I love how Lawler goes on to describe her feelings in that moment:

"I admired her and felt ashamed and stupid for sitting on the sidelines, covered up while my husband played with our kids. So I jumped up and ran into the water sprinklers to play with my kids. And as my clothing became soaked, I laughed at how silly I was for not wearing my bathing suit. I even said this to the mom at the water park. She smiled and said, 'It's okay. I understand.' We shared a knowing look, the look women share when we really understand one another. And I felt at peace, for the moment, with my body."

I love her transparency. She took words right out of my mind and heart that I have been too afraid to admit. That is precisely why I believe this book is a tremendous blessing for any mom who has been feeling "less than" or too afraid to admit she has been struggling for a long time.

Sweet Mama, we NEED this. We need honest conversation. We need to know that we aren't alone. We need to hear other mothers say they have been there, too, and they got through it.

Reading *A Letter for Every Mother* is like having a cup of coffee with a friend. It will perk you up and make you smile, but it will also move you to tears and give you the reassurance and encouragement you so desperately need to receive. Long and Lawler have created something extra special with *A Letter for Every Mother*. As a wife and mother of four little boys, and a blogger myself, I know that life can be super crazy at times. I loved reading these letters at the end of a hectic day—when I thought for sure that I had blown it—and finding that another mom had been there, too. Reader, you are certainly in for a treat with this book. So dive in, open your heart, and know that you are a valued part of the tribe on this amazing journey through motherhood.

# LETTER TO READERS

Our Dear Friends,

Thank you for buying this book and joining us here.

Some may call it fate, divine orchestration, or simply meant to be, but when we joined forces on what became this project, we knew with every fiber of our being that this was what we were called to do. Our mission was to create a book of letters for every mother, ones that would reach into your homes and hearts.

When we first connected, we realized our writing was similar enough to work beautifully together in a book, yet unique enough so one complements the other. As we continued to find that such a large part of our beliefs, values, and faith in God were incredibly aligned, we knew with certainty that some of our most favorite pieces should be made into letters and put in a collection together for readers. We have been blessed that our writing has touched and reached millions online; but in a world of constant virtual connection, we wanted to get back to basics. We wanted our letters to be in a format mothers could read together, beside one another. We wanted our letters to move beyond the computer to a book that could be held in your hands, given as a gift, and treasured as a guide. We decided to take some of our most beloved pieces and combine them into a book for every mother, grandmother, aunt, godmother, and mother-to-be, to find solace, humor, inspiration, and encouragement.

We want our words to join you on your sofa after the kids go to sleep. We want our book to help you to remember that we are all in this motherhood thing *together*. Our friends, we hope you read this book over and over again, and turn to a letter for support when you need it. We hope you pass our book on to a friend or give it as a gift to new or veteran moms who may need the same support. As you curl up with our book with a cup of coffee or glass of wine, we hope you find yourself here in the pages and know that you, our sweet friends, are not alone. We're here, holding your hand. This is the letter for every mother.

With love and gratitude,
Kara and Regan

I.

# COME, BE IN OUR TRIBE

*L*

With arms wide open, I open my door. The lights are on. Come, be in my tribe.

New mom, exhausted from an infant who doesn't sleep and needing rest, come, knock on my door. I can hold her while you sleep; it's nice and quiet in my guest room. I promise: This does get better, even though it feels like it never will. I've been there. I want to help you. Come, be in my tribe.

Working mom, with the career of your dreams, I know you sometimes feel rushed to get the kids after work. Let me pick them up for you and when you're finished with the meeting, swing by and get them. Come, be in my tribe.

Your youngest child is headed off to college in another month. Let's talk about your experiences. How did you do it? Sometimes, the days seem so long. Can you help me figure this all out? I need your advice. Please. Come, be in my tribe.

Stay-at-home mom, I know you mostly love being at home, but, sometimes, I think you crave a minute alone. I can take them to the park while you finally drink your cup of coffee, in peace. Really, I'm going to the park anyway. Come, be in my tribe.

Coworker with no kids of her own, I know it's loud and messy here, but I really love it when you stop over. I can make you a pumpkin spiced latte and we can talk about the books you've been reading. Come, be in my tribe.

Your maternity leave is over, so stop in if you can on your way to work. I will have chocolate and tissues waiting here for you, tied together with a turquoise bow. This day will be hard, but chocolate always makes me feel better. Come, be in my tribe.

Neighbor, sweet neighbor, I love how you enjoy my kids and how you look at me knowingly, with the soft smile of a grandmother. You tell me how quickly it all goes and I partially know, because my small children are growing so fast. I need your wisdom. Come, be in my tribe.

Former student, not a mom and maybe never a mom—the choice is all yours. My daughter loves to climb into your lap with her book. I think I can help you with papers and stories and life. And maybe you could help me remember that while I'm a mother and a wife, I was a teacher first. Come, be in my tribe.

Single mom, raising your kids and being on duty 24/7, I can take your son with mine for ice cream after baseball practice since your daughter has dance at the same time. Would that help? Come, be in my tribe.

Mom of two, whose husband is deployed, come and eat dinner with my family. It's the least we can do for your family's service. I'm really not much of a cook, but we could order a pizza and cut some fresh lettuce from my garden for a salad. Come, be in my tribe.

Women. Mothers. Friends. Sisters. Aunts. Grandmothers. Nieces. Cousins. It can be hard to find your tribe with true friends who surround you. But maybe it doesn't have to be hard? Let's come together. Let's be good to one another. It's really that simple. Reach out to one another. Come, start your tribe. Come, join my tribe. Come, be in my tribe.

# FOR THE MOM STARTING OVER

*L*

As we embrace a new year and a new season, what is one of the first things we do? We think of all the things we want to change or improve in our lives. We review and scrutinize all of the previous years' (or seasons') mistakes and short-comings, sometimes embarrassed or pretending they didn't even happen, and try to see them from our own perspective, rather than what is reality.

Nevertheless, it's a time when almost all of us revisit, review, and often criticize the choices we've made, where we have been, or maybe the places we have not yet traveled. This can be both a constructive and a demeaning ritual that we find ourselves practicing as each year draws to a close and a new year is blossoming right before us.

As mothers, we find ourselves thinking, *I wish I had more patience. Why do I lose my temper so often? I wish I would have spent more time with my children. Why didn't I follow through with the outings and trips I had planned for our family? I wish I wouldn't have said no so often and tried to listen a little more closely. Why have I not set a better example for my children in practicing what I preach?*

*I wish, I wish, I wish...Why, why, why...* We can keep beating ourselves up with these same questions as we play them over and over again in our heads or simply try to block them out and convince ourselves that we rock; we're the best mothers ever and make no mistakes. But the truth of the matter is, it doesn't change . . . any of it. Our past is nothing more than a story. Once we fully realize this, it loses its power over us. Accept it, learn from it, and move on. Trust me, it will be the best thing for both you and your children. There are far better things ahead than any we leave behind.

As we move into a new season, I've listed twelve aspirations to aim for as we continue to grow throughout the new year. If you are anything like me, you will fail miserably, possibly several times, at the tasks below, but pray to God you come out of it a better parent. One awesome thing we *do* have on our side is that every second of every day is a chance for us to start again. There are just days we choose to give up, give in, throw in the towel, choose to believe it's a bad *day* versus some bad *moments*. Instead, we need to pick ourselves up, dust ourselves off, and try again . . . right then, right there.

After all, this *is* a new year. A new season. A new start. With endless possibilities.

1. Forgive yourself, forgive your children for their mistakes, and forgive your partner for his mistakes. After examining and making peace with them, *move on*. We can't start the next chapter of our lives while we keep rereading the last one.
2. Think twice before letting "No" jump out of your mouth. The past cannot be changed, forgotten, edited, or

erased…it simply must be accepted. So many of those "No's" could easily have been a "Yes" if we would have only stopped and taken an extra two minutes.

3. Take a deep breath and slowly count to three. Remember, patience is a virtue. Patience *is* a virtue. I'm so grateful for the saying that every saint has a past and every sinner has a future. Thank You, God. There is still hope for me.

4. Remember, actions speak louder than words. *Be* the example of this.

5. Let your kids know you're human. They need to know that Mommy isn't a superhero…well, not all the time, anyway. Mommy makes mistakes. Mommy messes up. Mommy does things and says things that she wishes she hadn't. *But* Mommy also learns from her mistakes. She tries harder the next time. She doesn't give up. Mommy cries; she hurts and she has feelings, just like everybody else. It's important for your children to know this. So show them, or maybe on occasion reveal to them, this side of Mommy. Trust me, they will love you even more for it.

6. Let loose and be a kid, with your kid, every once in a while. You might have more fun than you think.

7. The dishes are stacked, the laundry is piled up, and dinner needs cooking, I understand that these tasks can't wait forever, although I think it's a wise decision to let them temporarily take a backseat at times, depending on the day and the attention your children need. But why

not include your children in your chores? Even if it's just for a couple of minutes, let them dry a dish, put a bowl away, help "throw" the clothes into the washer, or, my kids' favorite: "push the button." And all children love to help stir and pour in, to be the assistant chef. But most of all, they just want to feel important and feel included.

8. You can never have too many dance parties, you can never check on your children too many times throughout the night (no matter how old they are), you can never laugh too often, and you can never love too hard. Let yourself overdo some of these overdoable things. Once the moment is gone, it's gone.

9. When you start your day off exhausted, not showered (again), unorganized, and feeling like you're going to crumble to pieces, take five minutes to pull yourself together. Lock yourself in the bathroom, hide in the closet, stay an extra five minutes in the car (alone). Take some deep breaths. Regroup as best you can. And if you're like me, thinking to yourself that you're already running late to work and don't have those long, extra five minutes, then make sure to take them as soon as you can, when time allows. You'll be amazed by all that can be accomplished in five minutes after having a baby!

10. Each one of us has something in life that keeps us going, that keeps us looking forward to another day. Remember who your "somethings" are. Tell them that. Show them that. Then repeat again and again and again.

11. Say "I love you" until you think you've worn it out (which I hope for you will be *never*). A child can never be told that

you love them too often. But don't forget to not only tell them this, but to also show them. Reread #4 and realize how critical it is that these go hand in hand.

12. Be good to *you*. Love yourself enough to take a small amount of time out of *each* day to breathe, to just "be." Trust me, you deserve it more than you think. And you know what? You might just be a better parent for it tomorrow.

Look at this new season as a rebirth. Create the version of you that you want to be. You have a blank page before you. So write a good one.

# TO THE MOTHER-TO-BE WHO HATES PREGNANCY

*L*

Day after day, week after week, month after month. And yes, pound after pound. This journey continues.

It seems that as soon as I'm able to clear one hurdle, a new one surfaces. It is safe to say that I have made it out of the dreadful series of several months of headaches that would spike and turn into migraines, leaving me trying to function on a daily basis while not being able to hold my head up.

And yes, I should be thanking my lucky stars that I am not spending my days thinking that I need to have a garbage can or a bathroom within arm's reach.

However, the baby is now lying upon my sciatic nerve, which, at times, leaves me paralyzed in pain.

My breathing is heavier, as I have put on a decent amount of weight and the baby is pressing up against my lungs. There are days when I feel at least a decade older than I actually am.

I look at myself in the mirror and at times all I see is everything big and out of place that shouldn't be. Pregnancy is a growing process, and it seems that every other inch of me is trying to keep up with this continual development.

The daily *concerned* comments of, "Oh, you poor thing. You look terrible. Just exhausted. How are you even feeling?" Or one of my favorites that I receive in public: "Oh, my, look at you! You must be due any day now, right?" And I prepare myself for the jaw-dropping look I'll get when I tell them how much time I actually have left.

Selfishly, I miss my once-toned, muscular, fit body that now has officially turned to fatigued, soft rolls, and thickness…everywhere.

I laugh, I pee. I sneeze, I pee. I cough, I pee. Yes, it's just what I do.

I will be delivering at the very **end** of the summer. Need I say more?

As I never know which personality or mood is going to spring up from hour to hour, I mercilessly beg that this roller-coaster ride will fast-forward to a safe and healthy end. But as reality overtakes me, I am brought back to the fact that I have four months to clamber on.

My feet drag some days. On others, I find that they stomp, as only a two-year-old would do. And to keep pushing through my evenings past dinnertime, seems as if I am trying to finish the last leg of a marathon.

I find myself laughing and crying at the same time, and, on occasion, I'm not even really sure why.

*Sleep.* Such a beautiful word. Unfortunately, one that I can't use positively in my vocabulary. I learned after my first pregnancy that I had entered a matter of decades of this being a luxury of the past. If I'm not up with one of the other children crying for Mommy, I'm up to pee every other hour. Sadly, going to the bathroom twenty times a day has become nothing less than a chore.

But then . . . struggle after struggle, day after day, hour after hour, what is the one, or should I say *several*, saving graces that get me through all of this?

I catch myself smiling as I feel her kick and spin at the most unexpected times, and I'm once again reminded that **life** is inside me. For this being my fourth go at being pregnant, the novelty has yet to wear off.

I get to see my children ever so gently place their hands around my stomach while they kiss, touch, and talk to this new tiny person that will soon be joining us.

To see how much *they* already love her certainly may be one of my favorite parts of this entire experience.

I think of the captivating, life-changing, pivotal moment when they will lay her on my chest. To think I get to experience this most empowering ecstasy again . . . of *my* bringing a life into this world, is simply incredible.

I think of listening to the sounds when my baby will eat, of holding her close while she nurses. To call it bonding time is a colossal understatement. The irreproducible sounds of her taking the tiniest gulps of nourishment while being soothed and pleased is purely endearing, to say the least.

I think of holding and snuggling my baby as she lies on my chest, curled into my neck, while she takes the most delicate, tiny breaths into my ear. Again, a sound that could make a mother's heart beat right through her chest; a sound so precious and distinct, it's as if God's breath is still apparent upon this heavenly sent angel.

I think of the time her eyes will lock with mine, as soon as she will be able to clearly focus them, and to see, for the first time . . . the person in this world who would walk to the ends of the earth for her. The moment she actually *meets* and *discovers* Mommy.

I think of the time she will outstretch her delicate hand to wrap her tiny fingers around my own.

I think of the time she will cry for me, and although my body and mind will be physically and mentally drained, I will rush to her because it will already be instinct to answer her call.

I think of getting the comments about glowing and beaming with pride, looking past the wrinkles, gray hair, and bags under my eyes that will surely be visible. And how my never-ending love for this new, perfect little person will outshine everything. All of these hardships are only temporary, and although at times they seem never-ending, they amount to such a short lapse of time compared to the decades, God willing, that I will get to spend with her and watch her grow.

I think that no matter how tough of a pregnancy I have endured, and no matter what remarks I have irritably stated at the end of never going through this again, it is a matter of days after delivering that my body yearns for this experience all over again.

Each day brings a new humbling yet exalting experience.

How is it possible that I am distressed and delighted at

the very same time? How is it that as I find myself ready to crumble and feel so heavily burdened, I am snapped back to reality and understand the blessing that has been bestowed upon me?

The answer is simple: I am experiencing one of life's greatest miracles. *I* was chosen out of the other billions of women on this earth to be *this* little girl's mother.

# TO MY FELLOW STRUGGLING MOTHERS

*L*

There are days when everyone needs and wants to be held and there isn't a second I can find to myself. At all times, one of the children in the group is either unhappy, throwing a tantrum, crying, or shrieking. And I think, *Please, go play. Mommy needs a break. Just two minutes to myself. I can't hold you right now. My arms are about to break.*

I know some day I will want each moment back that I took for granted—and be begging for the opportunity to chase one of my children down, to have them let me hold them *at all.*

The incessant *one mores*—when I'm asked to color one more picture, read one more book, or play one more game after the previous hours of devoting every last breath of energy left in my body—find me answering at times with a slouch and a sigh.

Yet I know there will come a time when I'd give anything to be able to sit down and do these things not only one more time, but a thousand more times. There are mornings, afternoons, and evenings when I feel like a slave in my own kitchen. When it feels like it's more of a war zone. I don't get to sit down, because someone always needs another refill, a second helping—or, naturally, there is a mess that needs immediate attention.

And yes, *one* day, I will look around my kitchen and wish for it to be filled with little people who need me to wait on them hand and foot. All too soon, it will be empty and quiet.

There are moments when I feel like I can't change one more diaper, help one more time on the potty, wipe one more messy mouth, or clean up one more disaster. As soon as I get one of these tasks accomplished, the next is already waiting for me. But I know that ultimately, my need *to be needed* is far greater than anything else. Not only will I miss this, but I will *yearn* for it one day.

There are nights when the babies just won't go down for bed...or, for that matter, stay asleep. The times they prolong the inevitable at tuck-ins and ask for one more kiss, one more hug, one more drink of water, or have just one more thing to tell you...for the fifteenth time.

There will come a time when I would give *anything* to have made sure I took each one of those extra hugs and kisses and realize that I'm pacing the halls with an emptiness that can't be replaced.

Hundreds of times daily I hear, "Mommy, look! Mommy, just watch me! Mommy...Mommy? Come here! Mommy, can you help me with this?" There are times I think I could crumble and often, at my breaking point, I wonder: *How is it possible for one human being to meet all of these tiny people's needs all at once, every single day, all day and all night long?* I feel so defeated at times simply because there aren't five of me to go around.

One day, I will be praying to have those requests and sweet demands back.

There are never-ending pleas for me to watch the same show or movie over and over or listen to the same songs again and again. At times, my head aches and spins from it, and I'm certain it will burst if I see or hear something one more time. I realize at times that my much needed adult social vices are no longer met; they're simply a thing of the past.

But *yes*, at some point, I *will* laugh to myself and want it back.

There are ever-too-early awakenings when I'd give *anything* to have my kids sleep in and not have each day begin at 65 mph by 5:30 a.m. Most days, when I'm trying to get my eyes to open and remind my legs to put themselves one in front of the other, I'm not sure which direction I'm heading or what needs to be done first. I'm just doing a head count to make sure everyone is accounted for and made it through another night.

But this, *too*, will be one of those exhausting times that I will look back on and smile and think: *They were my reason to carry on and pull myself out of bed every day.* I will reach a point where I *need* to have these mornings again.

Someone is playing peekaboo during my two-minute shower and I hear squeals along with thumping feet running through our halls till it sounds like someone is being seriously hurt and our house will surely come crashing down.

One day, the peace and silence will be deafening. I *will* miss this.

There is the rushing from one event and appointment to the next. The constant in and out of the car seats to keep up with our schedule. And while we're traveling, the unremitting battles in the backseat that are sometimes enough to make it impossible to even attempt to drive safely. So often I think to myself that I must be one of the most courageous people on this earth to put these tiny people in the car and take all of them out in public by myself.

One day, I will turn around and find complete emptiness, with no one asking or needing me to take them anywhere or pick them up. I surely will want it all back.

The daily cleaning of the toothpaste out of the sink, switching the shoes that are on the wrong feet, fixing the shirts that are misbuttoned, keeping up with the never-ending loads of laundry, tripping over and picking up the sea of toys that lay scattered through the house, or once again scrubbing the crayon that has found its way onto a wall.

Yes, *all* of this, every single last thing: I will want it *all* back.

That's the crazy thing about motherhood—the most tiring and sometimes most dreadful duties are actually where we find the biggest hidden blessings.

The days of *Help, Mommy . . . Mommy, please . . . Just one more!* I need to at times beg myself to embrace this, all of this . . . the struggles, the exhaustion, the wearing of the fifty different hats to just survive one day with my little ones because one day, this will all begin to slow down and eventually come to a complete stop. There is no pause button. There is no rewind button. And, unfortunately, there is no *do-over* button.

In our moments of exhaustion and despair when we wish, *Oh, I can't wait until they're older. We just have to bear it a little longer to make it through **this** stage.*

There will come a time when I will feel sick just to think that I could have wished any amount of time away, when I would walk to the ends of the earth to be back *here*—right here, right now.

I'm given *one* shot with my children. They are given *one* childhood with me. The amazing, yet scary part of all of this is that *I'm* the author of this part of their lives. *I* determine how their chapters are being written out. Every day, I will go down in flames trying to give them memories that will allow them to look back one day and say, "I remember being *happy*. When I think of my childhood, I simply remember happiness."

And if I'm really lucky enough, they will know in their hearts that their mother, well, *she* was a huge contributor to that happiness.

As I fail and at times wish I could take my words or actions back, I simply must try to learn from my mistakes, hoping they made me a better parent.

Thank God, every day we're given a brand-new page to write on. Make today a good one.

# TO THE MOM ON THE SIDELINES AT THE WATER PARK

*L*

Today, I headed to a local lake with my children, and I was reminded of how far I've come. It was cloudy but as we shuffled to our spot on the beach, the clouds cleared and the sun revealed itself, in all its glory. Small bodies were lathered with sunscreen, heads were covered in colorful hats, and flotation devices were affixed. It was hot and I didn't hesitate for a minute to take off my own shorts and walk to the water with my daughter in just my one-piece bathing suit. This might sound normal but two years ago I wouldn't have been caught dead in a bathing suit.

That is, until the day I met a mom at a water park. She changed the way I thought of myself. It was a hot day, well over 90 degrees with the summer sun high in the sky. To escape the heat of the day, my husband and I took our kids to a small water park, one with a huge bucket, poised and ready to dump gallons of water on small faces, filled with pure delight, that wait underneath in expectation.

My baby girl was not quite a year old then, and I, embarrassed about my squishy stomach (and a body a restaurant server referred to as "big-boned" just the day before), put on a skirt and tank top. That server's words—the words of another mother, no less—rang in my mind as I chose what to wear that afternoon. Her words were like a match, lighting a new fire of self-doubt—and I felt consumed by it.

But then we got to the water park, and I saw another mother there, in her navy blue and turquoise bathing suit, running and playing with her two small boys. I saw her stand under that giant bucket of water with them. I saw her play in the fountains and toss her head in laughter. I saw her, not caring at all about what anyone else thought. I admired her and felt ashamed and stupid for sitting on the sidelines, covered up while my husband played with our kids.

So I jumped up and ran into the water sprinklers to play with my kids. And as my clothing became soaked, I laughed at how silly I was for not wearing my bathing suit. I even said this to the mom at the water park. She smiled and said, "It's okay. I understand." We shared a knowing look, the look women share when we really understand one another. And I felt at peace, for the moment, with my body.

Listen, I have a daughter. I teach English at an all-girls' school. And I want these girls of mine—daughter and students alike—to know that their bodies are the homes of their souls and their minds. For each, her body is simply a vessel for the woman she is. Our cellulite, our stretch marks—for some of us, the signs that we're mothers—are just outer marks on bodies and minds that have done some hard work.

No more will I sit on the sidelines because I'm insecure. And so I bought a swimsuit I really like and I get in the water because I don't want my own daughter ever to think twice about doing the same thing. And it's no coincidence that my daughter's new bathing suit has butterflies on it, just like the one she was wearing two years ago at the water park. That day, we saw a small butterfly fly through the concrete jungle of the water park. I won't ever forget the symbol, as butter-flies signify change. And today, I remember the changes I've made, and wear my bathing suit with pride.

# DEAR FRIEND: YOU ARE ENOUGH

*L*

I think you need to hear this today: You are enough. You are enough. You are enough. Can you take a deep breath and repeat this to me? *I am enough. I am enough. I am enough.*

You're all your child needs. You're all your partner needs. You're all your friends need. You're all your parents need. You're all your siblings need. You're all your job needs. You are a fantastic mother, partner, sister, daughter, friend, and worker, and you are doing enough.

You are doing enough for your children—loving her, loving him, loving them. Your children are safe, healthy, and happy, and on the days when they aren't, you do your best to make sure they return to being safe, healthy, and happy. We live in a day and age where we sometimes feel as if we are not enough and we're not doing enough. We rush to play groups, music lessons, summer camps, dance lessons, baseball practice, and library outings. We feel guilty that we are not doing enough. Is she eating enough good food? Did I breast-feed long enough? Am I reading to him enough? Is the school he's in good enough? Did I say enough about how much I love her? Did I relay to him enough how important he is to us? Does he feel safe enough and ready enough to venture into the world without me? Is she sleeping enough? Are we traveling enough? Are we exposing them to enough? Is there enough money to get them all they need? Am I home enough? Am I present enough? Am I doing enough? Am I a good enough example?

We take classes to continue our own education; we are done with our schooling; we never continued our formal education at all. We work outside the home full-time; we work part-time; we are stay-at-home moms. We help to care for our parents; we help our friends with their kids; we help even when maybe we shouldn't. We make homemade bread; we make friends; we make enemies; we make jelly so our children have their favorite jam for their toast. We speak with great thought; we speak without thinking; we speak too little; we speak too much. We mail presents; we mail letters; we mail bills. We plan board meetings; we plan Pinterest-worthy birthday parties; we plan lessons; we plan for our futures. We rush to get a run in; we rush to work; we rush to the store. We attempt to have wine with friends; we attempt to shower in peace; we attempt to sit on the couch for just five minutes to read a book that we started a month ago and still have not finished. We try to put laundry away for days; we try to make it to our big presentation on time; we try to be supportive of our friends. We run houses; we run companies; we run ourselves into the ground. We are confident; we are strong; we are insecure; we are many things in many forms. All the while, there are some days, like today, when we feel like we're not enough.

But, my friend. I know this: *You are enough.* Pass it on.

Isn't it amazing that we find inspiration in the most surprising places at times when we are least expecting it, but, fortunately, when we are needing it the most?

A few weeks ago, shortly into a shopping trip at Walmart, I could hear a child struggling. He was screaming, throwing some major temper tantrums, and when he came into vision, I could see that he was almost bucking himself right out of his seat in the cart. A poor toddler was beside him.

However, his mother was unusually calm; she almost had an odd sense of peace about her. She smiled. And I say "odd" only because it was uncanny how she kept herself so powerfully composed.

Despite her son's incessant outbursts, she continued to do her shopping, a decision that many obviously thought was wrong. If looks could kill, this poor mother would have been finished, right then and there. As our paths kept crossing in almost every aisle, I was mortified for her for a number of reasons.

I've been there myself, all too many times. We all have. When I take all of my children grocery shopping alone and manage to survive, I consider it a huge feat. Normally, it's never pretty, and although the parenting experts that be say you should immediately remove your child from the store to show them you won't tolerate their inappropriate behavior, doing so is not always an option.

For some, this is our only opportunity to get our family's groceries and we must push through the agonizing shopping trip, whether it is a pleasant experience for all or not.

Each glare I saw her receive—not to mention the few appalled whispers I caught—made my heart just break for her. I, too, have been the recipient of those evil looks and felt as if I were ready to crumble and wanted to hide in the first corner I could find.

For some reason, I was completely drawn to this woman. As people sneered and looked down upon her, their eyes asking, *How dare you let your son ruin my shopping trip!* I looked at her in total admiration. I thank God that I was able to notice what everyone else seemed to miss.

There were times the mother did calmly intervene when necessary. However, when it was appropriate, she let him express himself in the only way this sweet angel knew how. And what others failed to miss was the handful of times I saw her stopping to go over picture cards with him, showing him that soon they would be going home. Her otherworldly gracefulness and patience left me with chills.

Here I am, trying with all my might to hold one of my toddlers safely in the cart as she almost climbs out of her buckled seat belt, bribing the other toddler that if he is a good boy and stops touching and pulling things off the shelves, he'll earn his fruit snacks in the car (great parenting, right?), and coaxing my oldest to just give Mommy a few more minutes and to hold on to the cart, though her legs are too tired from walking and she's begging me to carry her. Was I a picture of grace and beauty? Hardly.

Before my encounter with this woman, I had recently started specifically seeking out and praying for more patience. It is something I have always prayed for and even joked about, but I truly felt convinced that this was, and still is, an area of my life that needs some serious attention and improvement. I felt a deep conviction to better myself with regard to my level of patience, although I've yet to find the magic ingredient for sustaining this concept. On some days, it seems simply impossible, and I think to myself, *If Mother Teresa or the pope were here, I just wonder with every ounce of me if they would be holding it together with the circus that is going on.*

But it was at the most appropriate time that I was, I felt, led to this woman.

Not only did we cross paths in several aisles, but it turned out that I was right behind her in the checkout line. Without even hesitating, I went up behind her, softly put my hand on her back, and told her I thought she was an incredible mother. With the most surprised, yet warmest smile, she immediately burst into tears. I think that was probably the last thing she expected to hear at the end of her shopping trip, yet it was probably something she deserved to hear from anyone who took the time to see the phenomenal things she was actually doing.

She introduced me to her son and briefly shared some of the struggles they faced on a daily basis with autism. I felt humbled to just be in their presence, and to be permitted to meet such a handsome, bright-eyed, intelligent young man. It's truly amazing how God facilitates such perfect timing in our lives when we least expect it. I left my grocery trip feeling more inspired as a mother than I had in the longest time.

After our few minutes of sharing and talking were over, we parted ways in tears. The mother thanked me for reaching out to her and shared that my feedback was not the type she normally received. I assured her that she was a blessing in disguise, a walking example of true perseverance, sincere compassion, and an overabundance of patience that left me in awe of her.

How often do we catch ourselves being so quick to judge? Especially in the cynical and competitive society we live in? As mothers we want to be the best, and we want our children to be the best, and if and when we're and they're not, we twist and conceive thoughts and make excuses in our heads until we believe what actually, in fact, is not reality. I feel bad for each person, especially each parent, who crossed paths with this mother and didn't get to truly see and experience and leave with the inspiration that I received.

I constantly look to be inspired, to find people or situations to improve my outlook on life and encourage me to become a better person. I think of the countless times I was not in tune or open to the hundreds of learning moments that I was right smack in the middle of but resistant to, just too busy to even notice, or found myself in total shut-down mode.

Life is simply about moments. We will remember not the days, but rather the moments that impact and change our lives. Luckily for us, these moments are all around us, waiting to be discovered and experienced. The hard part is already done. All that is left on our part is to live with our hearts and eyes wide open.

Miracles come in moments. Be ready and willing.

# TO THE BIGGEST FAN

*L*

This past weekend, we went to a local state park for a benefit walk and while there, I had a very honest exchange with a sweet little girl. The conversation left me wondering, all week, what could be gained if we spread more love around with smiles and compliments.

It was windy and cold on Sunday morning; fall had certainly arrived here in Pennsylvania, and we were all bundled up. The kids were excited, but my husband and I had gotten into a debate about what kind of clothing was appropriate for them. He's super relaxed about clothing and doesn't worry much about weather. I, on the other hand, kept asking him if our kids would be cold. We discussed this fact on the way to the park, and after a brief argument, I ended up feeling ridiculous for being the worrier in our little family. My list of questions included: "Does she need sunscreen? Where are their hats? Geez, it's cold. I hope they don't need coats." I was truly caught up in making sure they were warm and protected, and while that's not a bad thing, I guess, I did end up focusing on it a bit too much, losing out on the excitement of our morning. My husband, generally patient with me, was annoyed at my barrage of questions. And so we pulled into the parking lot of the park, with me feeling a bit undervalued and underappreciated and with my son saying, "Mama, you worry too much."

The wind hit me in the face and I immediately wished I had brought the hat for the baby. I didn't say this, however, because in the end, my husband would be right; she'd be fine in the backpack we had for her—protected on her daddy's back. My son ran off to play with friends on the dock, and my husband and I made our way down to the water's edge for the opening ceremonies. As the kids played, I walked around with my daughter, doing my best to listen to the speaker's words. The kids were gathering acorns, oblivious to the weather. I stared out at the water, tiny waves making the boats rock. No matter my worries, my kids were happy. And I continued to feel sheepish. My husband even joked with me, saying, "See, I told you. It's fine." And so I relaxed into the moment at the park, watching the kids gather the nuts.

There was one little girl there with big brown eyes and dark hair I had never met. I noticed her adventurous nature and her cowboy boots as she played with my son and the other kids. Minutes later, out of the blue, she came up to me and grabbed my hand. She told me her name and I told her mine. She looked up at me and said, "I'm a big fan." I was confused and asked her what she was a big fan of. She said, "You, of course." I just smiled, telling her how that was the sweetest thing I had ever heard. She squeezed my hand and smiled back. My eyes filled with tears at her simple statement.

All this week, I thought about her words and how they resonated with me at a time when I needed them. Kids are very honest. Adults could learn a lot about how to treat others from time spent with a small child.

This week, at various times, I spoke that little girl's words to my son: "I'm a big fan of that art project," or "I'm such a big fan of that Lego creation." One day, I told him I was a big fan of his new haircut, and that he looked awesome. His quick response was, "Thanks. I'm pretty sure that I do." Instead of feeling like I wasn't being genuine (which I was, of course!), he just accepted my compliment, confident in his own right and in the fact that I really am his big fan.

Let's go forth this week, spreading love, smiles, and compliments. You know, let's even smile and use those words, okay? "I'm a big fan." You never know how your heartfelt words will make a difference to someone who might need them.

# TO THE MOM WHO MISSES SUMMER

*L*

Is the end of summer hard for you?

At the end of the summer, I always miss sitting on the dock of the Chesapeake Bay from our time there during summer vacation. At the end of the summer, I always miss the lazy mornings playing on the porch in our pajamas. I miss the summer haze, the ice cream, the late nights playing until the sun sets. I miss the time we all spent with cousins and extended family. I miss the lake and the hikes in the woods and the way the rain seemed only to visit briefly because it knew the sun's glory could not be squelched. I miss it all.

I struggle during this time every year. Like the leaves that are beginning to change into brilliant reds and yellows or the way the crisp, mountain mornings now require a sweatshirt, the sadness returns and I sometimes fight back tears in my car after I've dropped the kids off at school. I miss summer even as I love the fall. Year after year, the struggle calls my name as my children and I return to school, schedules resume, and life becomes more rushed than I'd like it to be. And while I spend time dwelling on this (and shouldn't), today I was reminded of the gifts this time brings. Every year, as if on schedule, the gifts also arrive. Mamas, let's look at the gifts. It's hard sometimes, but if we look closely, they're right there for us to see.

On my daughter's first gym day, she had new sneakers to wear. They were navy with hearts on them and they lit up when she moved in them. She looked like Rainbow Bright in her outfit, and she was so proud. It was a gift watching her run in and show her teacher her new shoes, as she danced around so they would light up, her strawberry blond curls bouncing with her. It was a gift watching her hug her little best friend at school at the end of the day. It is a gift that she's happy and learning how to be a friend.

When I picked her back up, the older kids were on the playground. My son is 8, but that didn't stop him from running up to me, arms wide open, to give me a hug. And I hope this never ends, but I know it will—this unabashed hug in front of all the other kids. I'm telling you: This meant the world to me and it never would have happened if he wasn't at school—the hug likely would have but maybe not the realization that I must savor it.

Later, my son told me a story about one of his best friends—a little girl he's known since kindergarten. She got hurt on the playground and my son told me how he sat with her and checked on her. It's a small thing but it is everything in the end. I could see the pride on his face as he relayed the story. And I am so proud of him and the chance he had to make a decision to care for someone when he wasn't required to. This story wouldn't have happened if he wasn't at school.

That evening, my son played flag football—his first big

game. I watched attentively as he hustled, threw the ball, grabbed flags, and laughed with his friends. I never expected it, but right in the middle of the game, he stopped and looked at me, smiled, and waved. This never would have happened if he hadn't been back to school and with his classmates on a team.

There are more gifts. The reconnecting with the school communities where I work and the one where my kids attend—the laughter with some of my best friends when we wait to pick up the kids after school, the way a coworker told me I looked "so calm and peaceful" (it's an illusion, but I liked hearing it!), the hug from a school friend I haven't seen since May. These are all gifts this time of year brings.

And soon, I'll be welcoming my own students into my English classroom. There'll be so many gifts as a result of that. I spent today paging through a favorite book in preparation for their return. And that's a gift.

Change is sometimes hard, isn't it? I'd be lying if I told you that I didn't miss the snuggle mornings with my babies or the coffee on the porch as our rooster crows. I do miss it. I really do. But let us all try hard to celebrate the gifts because they're there, too. Every season has its own rewards. So, let's not miss summer, for it'll be there, as true as the water in the bay I love so much. It'll be there, waiting for us.

# FOR THE HATED, HOT MOM

*L*

Here she comes.

She's walking toward you, gorgeous smile, gorgeous hair, gorgeous figure (even after popping out a handful of kids), with a glowing aura about her. Admit it. You're secretly hating her, exhibiting a human flaw that not *all*, but *a lot* of women inherently possess—jealousy. It's not an attractive trait by any means. But for some, it's a secretly hidden attribute that brews ferociously inside them,

Why is it so easy to give the *"hot mom"* the eye roll as you turn to whisper to your partner or friend something nasty about her, most likely a woman you've never met? *"Just look at her. Who does she think she is? What good mom actually wears something like that?"*

Is it wrong for that mother to take pride in her personal appearance? Is it wrong for her to be fit? Or even wrong for her to *want* to look good?

Bottom line: A "beautiful" woman doesn't fit one mold of five foot two and 105 pounds, long blond hair, blue eyes, perfect teeth and smile, and fully accessorized in the best name-brand clothing line and shoes.

*Beautiful* is a smiling woman. *Beautiful* is healthy. *Beautiful* is confidence. *Beautiful* is strong. *Beautiful* is energetic. *Beautiful* is uplifting. *Beautiful* is inspiring. *Beautiful* is resilient. *Beautiful* is in the way she carries herself. *Beautiful* is in the way she doesn't let the trivial and unmindful pettiness affect her. *Beautiful* is in the way she understands the hard work it takes to have something, well…worth having. *Beautiful* is in the way she takes care of not only her family, but herself. Her emotional, spiritual, and, *yes*, physical well-being.

You know we've all heard it, laughed about it, and jokingly went along with it…but what truth it holds: *If Mama isn't happy, nobody in the family is.* All too often we do what we think is best in putting everyone else first, which, let's face it—is part of the job. But also all too often, we become the selfless martyr, bitter and resentful about everything we do for others and not taking any time to do something important for ourselves.

At the end of the day, **you** have to be happy with yourself before your partner, children, family, friends, acquaintances, or the next passer-by can fully enjoy the beautiful person you **are**, inside and out. Learning to love and accept ourselves, admit to our shortcomings, and take a step forward in bettering ourselves is not an easy task.

After becoming a wife and mother to multiple children, it was a hop, skip, and a jump to putting my own needs last. It's just what *had to be* to make everything else *work* and keep functioning. And then I realized I needed something for me. I realized I deserved it. I realized I was worth it. And so with sheer determination, complete and tireless motivation, and most importantly, believing in myself—that I was strong enough to do it—I decided to make some changes that would benefit not only myself, but my entire family.

Remember, *nothing* worth having comes easily. Step outside your comfort zone. Your fuel, your fight, your desire must be greater than your desire to stay the same.

Do something today that your future self is going to thank you for. How many other fad diets, tricks, and quick fixes have you tried? If the plan doesn't work, change your plan, *not* your goal. Do not be discouraged by the past attempts that didn't pan out.

One of my favorite quotes is from Walt Disney, a man who failed many times, had hundreds of doubters, and thousands of obstacles—to the point that it would have made sense for him to throw in the towel. He said: *"If you can dream it, you can do it."* Tell the naysayers to step aside and *watch* you do it. And quite honestly, your biggest opponent is going to be the one staring back at you in the mirror. It will be a learning process for "you both" as you wage internal and external battles. Despite that struggle, let the strong, empowering *you* win.

Don't just talk about it, *be* about it. Being the matriarch of the family holds so much responsibility, including setting an example of what being healthy *actually* means.

If you happen to be on the envious side of wishing you looked like someone else's beautiful, realize that you are *already* your own beautiful. We all come to a point where we may need to ask ourselves how we're presenting that to others.

What might need refinement or tuning up to get to your maximum potential? Remember, we're all moms. We're all on the same team. We're all works in progress to become the best versions of ourselves. And with that comes a lifelong commitment.

# A PETITION FOR THE WORKING MOM

*L*

Dear Mr. President,

Tomorrow, I will do the unthinkable. Once again, I will pass my newborn into someone else's hands. My heart will break, despite praying that I would not have to experience this pain for the fourth time.

I'm told to toughen up. I'm reminded that I should be thankful I have a job. I get told again and again that I have the easiest job of being a teacher and the best schedule that a working mother could hope for.

Yes, I have toughened up. Yes, I am thankful I have a job. And yes, I do have a wonderful schedule as a *working* mother. But here I am, preparing myself yet again to leave my very new baby with someone else.

Tomorrow morning, I will race around the house to ensure that I can do as much as possible for my children before leaving for work. And despite the fact that I am just one of hundreds of thousands of working mothers who must do what they have to do for their families, my heart breaks as I know they, too, are suffering and aching for their baby.

Hard work? I am not afraid of it. You could call me a "*mompreneur*," as I have started a photography business and a fitness business, embarked on a writing career, and also have a full-time job as a teacher. No, Mr. President, I am not afraid of hard work, nor do I pat myself on the back for working hard. Does this make me a great wife and mother? Does this make me an outstanding citizen and taxpayer? Does this put me in an elite category above others?

No. Not in the least.

It simply makes me a *decent* person. It shows that I will do whatever it takes to ensure that my family has what they need. I *do* feel blessed that I am able to contribute to keeping our family afloat.

We are your typical middle-class family. My husband and I both have good jobs. We work hard and we provide a roof over our four children's heads, warm beds to sleep in, and full tummies every night. Our children have everything they need; however, by the sheer grace of God, we just make it by each month after our mortgage, school loans, and bills are all paid.

But if you ask what our children want most, they'll tell you they want their *mommy*.

Tomorrow, I will wipe away tears, pull toddlers off my legs, unclench tiny arms from around my neck, and pass a very new baby over to someone else. I will not be able to kiss boo-boos that might happen throughout the day. I will not be able to lay the babies down for their naps. I will not be able to feed my newborn when she cries for me.

Once again, I will have to try to pretend Mommy isn't hurting or an emotional wreck inside and make my best attempt to put on a brave face for the sake of my babies. But knowing myself, no matter how courageous I strive to be, undoubtedly tears *will* stream down my face. My children *will* see the pain in my eyes. Despite my best efforts and complete preparation, tomorrow morning *will* be terrible.

Tomorrow morning, I will walk out my front door only to look back at tearful faces in the window and hear the baby crying behind the door. It will be all I can do to put one foot in front of the other, open the car door, put the key in the ignition, and drive away to work. Then I will have twenty-plus second graders waiting for me to inspire, love, and educate them.

Despite the absolute crushing pain I'll be feeling inside—the emotional torment of leaving my newborn—I'll have to dig deep for superhuman strength and try to do what needs to be done.

You see, Mr. President, the baby is now holding her head up. She is smiling all the time, especially when she hears my voice or I come into her view. Her eyes are just now starting to focus. Even though she is nine weeks old, just a few weeks ago, she *met* Mommy for the *first* time. Her eyes locked on mine and we *met*.

It was in that one moment she recognized that I'm the one who is there for her as she wakes throughout the night. I'm the one who rushes to her at the first unhappy sound she makes. It's my chest on which she lays and immediately calms and my neck she cuddles her tiny, perfect head into. Yes, she now knows just who *Mommy* is. And tomorrow, all too quickly, I must leave her.

I have such trouble wrapping my head around the thought and accepting the fact that we don't have a paid maternity leave applicable to us. We are not given a fighting shot to be able to stay afloat while getting the critical bonding time with our babies that both our children and we as mothers *need*.

Tomorrow, I will miss the bonding experience that comes with nursing my baby. Instead, she will struggle to eat (she doesn't do well with the bottle), and I will rush to find time in my hectic day to pump for her in the corner of the nurse's office. The thought of this alone makes my heart hurt and my frustrations rise.

So I ask you, Mr. President, why is the United States the only developed country without laws providing paid maternity leave? In fact, why are we one of the only countries without *any* paid family leave?

This baby that I will pass over tomorrow morning is my fourth baby... my *last* baby. I had prayed that by this point things would be different, that I could be home longer to nurture her throughout the day. To hug her, and rock her, and kiss her, and hold her as often and as much as I pleased. To bond with her and nurture her in a way that only her mother can. But that is not the case.

As one mother speaking on behalf of hundreds of thousands of hardworking mothers, please *protect* this vital time for a mother and her newborn. *Protect* and respect this grace period that is so critical in ways I can't begin to list or count.

Tomorrow, I will do the unthinkable. Somehow, someway, I will join the thousands of other women who have to pass their newborn over to other arms, walk away, and attempt to be the gladiators we are.

But Mr. President, wouldn't it be nice if we didn't have to be gladiators... *just yet*?

We've all been there, and if you haven't been there just yet, you'll soon know what I'm talking about when you're in that spot and the panic button gets... **pushed**.

The baby won't stop crying. Holy freaking crap. You love this little human being more than life itself, but you would probably even stand on your head right about now to get them to stop the tears.

So when you feel like you've tried it all, make sure you eliminate all of these "go-tos" below.

If you're a seasoned parent, you will read these and laugh and shake your head, thinking: *Yep, been there, done that, and after three and a half hours of excruciating crying, one of these actually worked.*

1.  Give them a bag of toilet paper rolls, a box of tissues, an empty water bottle, a remote control (the remote control is always a sure winner), or something that makes absolutely *no sense* for them to have fun playing with. If they can't choke on it and it can't poison them, by all means, just give it to them. GIVE IT TO THEM. You wouldn't find it in the baby section at the store? Who cares. Hand it over anyway.

2. Think of the most embarrassing voices and noises you can make. Get your "fun character" game voice on, take them outside, and in that high-pitched baby voice, point to everything (things that aren't even really there but, well, could be there). Like, "*Oh my goodness! Look at the bird. Where's the birdy? Do you see the bunny? The squirrel... look at the squirrel, honey!*" (As you pray to sweet Jesus that the darn squirrel appears since you see them every other hour of the day you walk out the front door.) Who cares that the neighbors wonder why in the world you're talking like that or pointing to invisible things. You're desperate. And wait... do you hear that? Did the baby stop crying? Time for a Mommy victory dance!

3. Make an absolute fool of yourself. Hurt yourself. Babies love that. Stub your toe. Run your body *full on* into a door. Bounce your head off the cupboard. They will love it. Just know, as you're pretending, more than likely you're going to actually hurt yourself. Or who knows? You may get lucky and not have to act but instead actually trip over one of the toys that lay scattered throughout the house—a sore reminder of the hundreds of dollars you spent on all these flipping things that the baby doesn't even want to touch. Hurting yourself? **It works.** Classic go-to.

4. Find the weirdest object for your baby to chew on. If it doesn't make sense for them to want to gnaw on it, more than likely that'll be the thing to do the trick. My baby prefers old, dirty shoes to chew on, but hey, that's just how she rolls. One of the questions I'd love to ask God

when I get to heaven is, "Why can't babies be born with their teeth already through?" Instead, we become creative trying to get *baby-teething soothe-whisperers* added to our personal résumé. So once again, if that little sweet pea can't choke on it or ingest something harmful, good lawdy, just let them have at it.

5. Play peekaboo. Doesn't matter where you're at. Doesn't matter what you throw over your head. Just do it. And after you feel that you're losing wind and can't breathe after putting the flipping jacket, garbage bag, whatever the hell it may be, over your head one more blessed time, do it another sixteen times. And side note: The more ridiculous you look, the better job you're doing. Just . . . don't . . . stop.

6. Think of the most annoying baby show's beginning song and play it for them—singing it and bouncing them during the entire duration; then repeat about twenty-two times. By that time they may have forgotten why they were upset and crying in the first place. If all else fails, push rewind and just tell yourself, *Suck it up, buttercup. The baby isn't crying right now! What would you rather hear? Peppa Pig's intro or the baby screaming?* Choose carefully.

7. Put a bottle or boob in their mouth. That's my family's answer for everything. *The baby's crying, honey. Mommy, the baby wants to nurse. I think . . . I think the baby needs to eat.* Oh, yeah, what was I thinking? I just fed her about eight minutes ago, so naturally . . . yes, naturally, she would need to eat . . . again.

8. Let your baby play in goop. Something that will make a

complete and utter mess, something that you'll have to spend a large amount of time cleaning off of your hardwood floors or scrubbing out of your carpets. Who knows, their precious little outfit may be ruined and stained, but my God, they're happy! The tears have disappeared. Let them put it wherever the heck they want. Pay good money for the floor cleaners later. Totally worth every penny.

9.  Bang things together...creating as piercing a noise as possible. It will be both soothing and music to their ears—give them a pot and any dishware they can't hurt themselves with, along with spoons and ladles and stirrers to pound obnoxiously on anything and everything. If they can't do it themselves, yep...you guessed it. You're up to bat. You've become the rock star drummer and your audience awaits. Get to it, Mama!

10. Let them pull clothes out of a drawer. You will soon realize that all the time you spend folding laundry doesn't matter. Four children later, I no longer fold clothes. It's by the sheer grace of God that an item makes it out of the dryer and into the right drawer. So hold them next to a drawer that holds the dish towels, underwear, socks, whatever, and just let them pull everything and anything out. *A side note:* You may want to clear any fun clothing out of that drawer. Last time the baby pulled things from my underwear drawer, my toddler wore a pair of my thongs on his head, running about our house, asking why Mommy's underwear were all cut and pieces were missing from them. Yeah. All modesty right out the window.

Pure genius, right? How did it take me four babies to figure some of these out? All I know is that I will go down in flames...*flames*, making the biggest fool of myself whenever, wherever the incessant cries go off.

It's exhausting, absolutely debilitating some days, but hey...these tiny, perfect noisemakers are so, so worth it. There will come a day when I will think back, laugh, and with tears streaming down my cheeks, wish with everything in me to *just...go...back.*

II.

*L*

You. Me. Us. Them. We became mothers.

*"Did you have them naturally?"* she asked me when she heard that both of my babies were born at over nine pounds. I had my children vaginally, but I didn't have them without medication. My body formed my children, grew my children, and birthed my children, and yet, I'm never sure how to answer this question. Are they asking me if I had them vaginally? By C-section? With medicine? Without medicine? Regardless, I became a mother.

*"She took the easy way out,"* she said about a woman who had a C-section because her son was breech. In some cases, cesarean sections are life-or-death scenarios for the mother or the child. And if they are more a matter of convenience, there is nothing easy about having your belly cut open to deliver life. Her body formed her child, grew her child, and she also birthed her child. She simply has a scar to prove that she became a mother.

*"It's so sad she couldn't have her own,"* she commented about a mother who adopted her child. Genetically connected with the same skin, eye, and hair color or not, your children are

your own. There is nothing sad about what I see in the eyes of an adoptive mother when she looks at her child. By adopting this child, she became a mother.

"*I knew she would cave!*" she declared about a strong-willed woman who had promised in her birth plan that she wouldn't accept medication during the birth of her child and had proclaimed to all that her body was made for labor. After fifteen hours of trying to follow her own proclamation, she asked for an epidural. Two hours later, her baby was born. She was crestfallen to go back on her own word, but it taught her that kids change almost everything; this is how she became a mother.

"*She is such a warrior,*" she said reverently about a mother who gave birth at home without medication. This warrior believed in the power of her body and it didn't fail her. She had an uncomplicated childbirth, void of any medication. Mothers are warriors: warriors of love and light for our little ones, brought into the world in whatever way we could. And this strong warrior became a mother.

"*She just didn't want to be pregnant anymore,*" she commented about a woman who was induced two days before her due date. What she doesn't know is that the woman's blood pressure went sky high and an induction saved both her life and the life of her daughter. Induced to guard the health of them both, she became a mother.

"*Is she your biological daughter?*" she asked me when I was recently out shopping with my redheaded daughter (I'm a brunette). She is my biological child; however, biological or not, she's my baby and I'm her mother. And all the women who have had children in alternate ways—with an egg donor or through some other method—became mothers.

"*She shouldn't have a VBAC*," she decided about a friend who had a C-section with her first baby but was trying for a vaginal with her second. But the mother wanted to try for a vaginal birth, and the second time around, she beat the odds and was successful. No matter that each birth was different, the end result was the same: She became a mother.

"*She fell apart*," she said in judgment of the woman who was crying and screaming and swearing when he was born. She was exhausted and overwhelmed and terrified. She fell apart, and in the falling apart, she became whole. It might not have been pretty, but she became a mother.

"*I didn't get to hold her right away*," she told me about the birth of her daughter. Her labor was difficult, and the baby was whisked away for treatment after swallowing meconium. She might always remember how she wanted to hold her baby immediately after birth, but first and most important, she will remember that she became a mother.

You. Me. Us. Them. We became mothers. It doesn't matter how we became mothers; it only matters that we became mothers. Let go of the divisions that separate us and let's be mothers together—mothering our children together and lifting our spirits together. Lord knows, we need the support!

We were stuck inside all day as the skies were unleashed. The rain fell heavily as we watched from the window and then from under the shelter of our front porch. The kids sat on the front steps, reaching a hand or stretching a foot to catch a raindrop. They giggled as the rain wreaked havoc on the trees, the leaves bowing under the weight of the downpour. We moved back and forth, back and forth—from the front porch to the house—all day long, as we waited and waited for the rain to stop. All I could think about was how to pass the time until the storm was over.

Since we couldn't go outside to the bright blue kiddie pool we have in our small backyard, the kids got in the tub and played with toys and bubbles, kicking to "Splish, Splash," on the radio. My one-year-old daughter learned how to kick her feet, and my son and I laughed as we watched her raise her foot, quite deliberately, and then bring it down again. She echoed "One, two, three," and then kicked, splashing water. It was still raining when the bath fun was over.

We made peanut butter and marshmallow fluff sandwiches and my daughter marveled at this new white substance, her small lips outlined with white. When I put the jar away in a cabinet within her chubby arm's reach, she quickly opened the cabinet door to retrieve it. Her new love is marshmallow fluff, and I just can't apologize for that being my one-year-old's new obsession. And the rain continued to pour down.

So we danced. Boy, did we dance! We tuned in *Uptown Funk* on the radio, and my son ran to retrieve sunglasses for us all. Mimicking the dancers from the music video, all three of us danced around the living room. Next, we gathered all the blankets we could and made a huge living room fort—the first time the three of us had done that. The kids crawled through it and rolled around underneath it, but my one-year-old couldn't resist wrecking it. It wasn't long before it was just a huge pile of blankets, but the building and the demolition passed a good thirty minutes.

For a second, it felt like winter—with the cool air of the air conditioner coming through the soft blankets. The humid air hitting us in the face as we opened our front door to check on the storm reminded us, though, that this was a summer storm, and it was not done.

All day long, we wanted the rain to stop. Rain on a summer day can seem unfair. But in the passing of the day, we made memories, just the three of us. My daughter learned how to splash with her feet and ate marshmallow fluff. We danced. We made blanket forts together for the first time. Wishing the time away was missing the beauty of these special moments, these *fleeting* moments.

After the rain stopped, we were left with flooded sidewalks, sidewalks that are so uneven, just the previous evening I had been complaining about them to my husband. My son took my daughter's hand and walked her down the sidewalk, helping her to wade through her first rain puddle. And as I watched my children, finally outside after a day of fun inside, I was so happy for the flooded sidewalks that I rolled up my pants and waded in the rain puddle with them.

# TO EVERY FIRST-TIME PARENT

*L*

I just had a few moments alone with my fourth baby who recently turned ten months old. We were playing on my bed and as she used the wall to brace herself, she turned around and waved to me. A real wave for the first time. She was giggling and beaming as she could tell by my reaction that she was doing something she should be proud of.

My eyes brimmed with tears. My throat cracked as I squealed with pure delight, and it amazed me that as I stared at my fourth child, those firsts still took my breath away... literally. I scooped her up in my arms and kissed her cheeks about fifty times as she laughed, before she began pulling away from me so she could stand up to wave at me again.

And then it dawned on me.

As all of her little first moments were flashing before my eyes, I hadn't marked down a single one of them. I hadn't even started a scrapbook yet, for that matter. What the hell kind of mother am I to let all of these treasured milestones simply pass by without even being documented on a baby's first-year calendar or in a scrapbook?

I still look back and recall late nights of frustration after having my first baby, not due to her, but because I had put so much pressure on myself with all these things I felt that I *needed* to do for her. I remember I was documenting the first time she tried a certain taste of food. Her first visit to a park. The first time she fell and got a bruise on her tiny knee. I swear, the first time she blinked or lifted her head, it was probably written down somewhere.

Granted, I loved scrapbooking and keeping these special photos and moments for her, but it started to become more of an obligation, a pressure that I put upon myself. By the time I had my second baby, I was struggling to keep up the recording of the keepsakes while still keeping my sanity. Then, following suit every other year, baby number three came. I know I had bought some photo albums, but I don't believe the majority of them are even out of the packaging yet.

That being said, we had our fourth baby in six years. To say that things got chaotic is a rather large understatement. Not that I love this baby *any* less than my first, God knows that. And yes, I have certainly captured many photos and videos of not only her, but all of our children together that I will treasure forever.

However, some may think I fall into the *Slacker Mom* category because I can't tell you the exact date this baby rolled over. I can't tell you how old she was when she first stood unassisted. I can't remember what month she was when she first said "Mama" and "Dada." All right, I'll be honest: Right now I'm trying to remember if I showered yesterday or if it was the day before yesterday.

But I can tell you I was there. Yes, I was there for each milestone of hers, applauding like a wild woman, cheering and carrying on as if she were an Olympian winning a gold medal. I was able to hold her and squeeze her and love on her, giving her probably too many kisses (if that's even possible) and whispering "I love you" over and over again in her ear, my heart ready to burst with her first time crawling, her first time sitting up, the first time she was able to pick something up with her own tiny, precious fingers.

Yes, if I could turn back time, I would give myself a pat on the back (hell, maybe even a nice shoulder rub) and tell myself to just breathe. Relax. Enjoy the moments. To sleep when I can, which isn't often, but to not run myself into the ground trying to keep up with the status quo of attempting to be *Remarkable Mommy*.

I would tell myself that the photos from all the sessions that went awry are ten times better than the "perfect," boring, posed, forced-smile ones. I would whisper gently in my ear that it's good to have a schedule and attempt to be organized, but 9 times out of 10, plans will change. Instead, just roll with it when things don't happen that should have and things do happen that, well ... simply shouldn't.

I would not get bent out of shape because someone gives me their unsolicited two cents' worth. Instead, I'd smile politely and thank them, whether I agreed with their advice or not. I would remember that part of taking care of my family is taking care of myself. Instead of always playing the martyr, I'd *let* people help me. Take the thirty-minute nap when a family member offers to hold the baby. Let your friends make you a dinner. And when your husband tells you to take that run or drive to the mall alone...well, thank God...and take it.

I would put my phone and the camera down more and just *be* in the moment. I would try to enjoy the precious moments versus trying to capture a photo each second. I would remind myself that the laundry and the dishes and the dusting and cleaning will be waiting and piled up no matter how much attention I give them, and that work is just, well, that—work.

Each baby has been a learning experience. Four babies later and with seven and a half years of being a parent under my belt, I still find myself making some of the same mistakes and still struggling to find balance in it all.

But one thing I do know is that I'm all my babies ever want. Just *me*, my attention, my love, and my approval. And that, *that* I can do.

My children won't have the most organized mementos of photos and albums and scrapbooks and calendars that have everything orchestrated to a tee, but they *will* remember that Mommy was there, for all their moments, for all their milestones. That is what matters most.

# DEAR MAMA: THIS IS THE NEW NORMAL

*L*

A friend with a new baby recently told me that she was waiting for things to return to normal. It got me thinking about parenting and how things are never the same again. With the birth of a child comes the birth of a new normal. The normal changes from hour to hour, day by day, week by week. That's the thing about parenting: you think you're onto something and the game changes. But the really crazy thing about the new normal? You wouldn't actually have it any other way.

Normal used to be eight or more hours of uninterrupted sleep, coupled with naps on the weekends. The new normal is rarely getting a night of uninterrupted sleep and when you do, you panic and run to the child's room to make sure he or she is still breathing. Or, on nights you could be sleeping, you lie awake and watch them sleep. This new normal isn't so bad after all because it's tiny toes in your side or snoring in your arms. The sleep thing is one of the hardest parts of the new normal, but eventually (they say) it gets easier.

Normal used to be going out to dinner with your significant other. You'd dress up, maybe, or call friends to meet you. You would talk and laugh over dinner, eating your food while it was warm and enjoying every bite. The new normal? You might try to get a babysitter, to no avail, or maybe you decide on a family dinner. You pull your hair up into a ponytail and wipe the marker off of your face. You order chicken fingers and fries because that's what the kids like and it is the thing that comes the fastest from the kitchen. Your children have their own plates, but for some reason they insist upon eating from yours. You eat quickly, and rarely while it is hot. But as you watch them dip their French fries in ketchup and they giggle when they put some on your nose, you have to laugh, too.

Normal used to be long and regular shopping trips with your sister, mom, or best friend. You'd leisurely decide between the black or gray top, while sipping your latte. The new normal is a trip to the store on a Saturday night and watching (and laughing) as all the other parents end up there, too! You watch another family, much like your own, in line at the snack bar. As your daughter begs for a cookie, you hear their son begging for a slushy, not the organic juice the mom is pushing. Above their heads, you smile at one another and remember this tribe of women, silent sometimes, but united by experience of this new normal.

Normal used to be a house that was relatively tidy, usually company ready. The new normal is that your house is never ready for unannounced company but you're learning to welcome them anyway. You're learning to let go of those expectations and just say, "Come on in. The door is always open." So, the new normal is toys all over, crumbs on the floor despite the fact that you sweep often. It's handprints on the door or windows and pretzels on the sofa. But all of this shows that little people live here and grow here. They laugh here and play here.

Normal maybe used to be a life that was quieter. Books and movies on the sofa or long walks at your own pace. The new normal is louder. It's squeals and laughs and crying and whining. It's books and movies still, but mostly, they aren't of your choice. And walks are different now, too, because your son stops to talk to every dog and to show you every acorn. But he is an explorer and you remember that you are, too.

Mornings in the old normal might have been hurried, but it was only because you overslept. You took your time and actually got a shower and did your hair. You picked your clothes carefully and stopped for coffee on your way to work. You actually listened to the music you liked! The new normal is a morning of craziness and the morning shuffle. Maybe you still shower and do your hair, but it's always at a faster pace and most days, you just throw your hair in a ponytail. You grab a coffee through the drive thru and promptly spill it on yourself. You sing "Shake it Off" loudly on the way because your daughter laughs while you do.

And while sometimes you will visit the old normal, it won't be there to stay. Sure, you'll go on a date night or a shopping trip with your favorite women. Yes, you'll read your own books and watch movies you really want to see and sometimes, your house will be really clean! And you will enjoy those times a lot. Sometimes, you'll crave the old normal so badly, you'll run out of the house in your pajamas because another adult came home and you needed a break. But even when the old normal returns in the fleeting moments that it does, you'll always want the new normal back. You like your crazy life. Because for you, that's the way. It might not be the way for everyone and you know that's okay, too. But it is the way for you.

And as these kids of yours grow, the normal will shift again until eventually, the old normal will seemingly return. But even then, these children will always be there in your heart, even if they are in college or married or traveling the world. You will just adjust to the new normal, even if it's hard like it first was when you became a parent. The new normal or the old normal— you're just happy you were able to experience them. And we moms mother through whatever normal we're in.

# A NOTE TO THE MOTHER RUNNING ON FUMES

*L*

As a mother, no matter how many other jobs we have, no matter how many other "hats" we wear, we are officially on call 24 hours a day, 7 days a week, 365 days a year.

There are no sick days so we can call in for someone to take our place. There are no personal days we can prep for. It's us. We are the job. We push our limits on a daily basis until we can push no more. Then what?

We begin to travel and exist in cruise control and, may I add, do so very dangerously. We are there physically, but emotionally and mentally we have already checked out. Have you ever caught yourself driving in this frame of mind? But somehow, by the sheer grace of God, you made it safely to your destination, and have no clue how? You have no remembrance of barely getting yourself in the vehicle or turning the key. And if you had the children with you, my God, did you secure them properly? Did you actually read the exit signs to make your turns, stop at the red lights, and follow the hundreds of traffic laws while barely keeping an eye open at the wheel?

As mothers, we push ourselves to the max, because for the majority of the time, there is no other choice. We can cry about it, throw ourselves a little pity party, stomp our feet (come on, we all know we have done this on occasion), and complain until there's no one left within a mile's radius to hear us. But sadly, nothing changes. If anything, we've just made the situation worse.

We go from one job to the next, meeting the requirements of the workforce, then answering the demands of our squadrons at home. There are times when it is physically hard to pick ourselves up and make it from one room to the next. Some moments call for mental coaching of trying to tell one leg to put itself in front of the other and cheering on our eyelids to stay open for, well, just a few more hours.

We are up all night whether it's feeding, consoling, or pacing the halls, but that doesn't mean we get to sleep all day.

We are drowning in urine, vomit, tears, and spit-up, but we still must kick and tread high, uncertain waters to stay afloat.

We are the doctor, lawyer, teacher, police officer, chef, chauffeur, maid, cheerleader, hair stylist, family therapist (even though most days, we personally need about four or five therapy sessions of our own), financial adviser, dental hygienist, spiritual leader, and, among the many other fabulous titles, household CEO.

When we find ourselves sulking in self-pity, tearing our hair out and fighting the incessant yawns from the sleepless night before, that is right when and where we must seek out the positives in each day, even if some days we must search harder. We vow to chase the mind-set that these challenges will only make us stronger.

To say that motherhood is a roller-coaster ride is an under-statement. One hour you are living on a high; you are proud, you are basking in your children's glory, and the world seems to be standing still as you are beyond overjoyed. The very next hour, as high as you were flying, you quickly come crashing down. It literally takes seconds to change the momentum of your day. The next thing you know, your focus is just to hang on tight and pray to God that you and, more importantly, the children, make it to bedtime. It's all you can do to remain some-what stable when you feel ready to explode, crumble to pieces, or lock yourself in the nearest closet, candy bar in hand, and sob yourself into a sweet slumber.

There are many days when we constantly question our-selves, continually doubt and tell ourselves that we can't, simply because there is nothing left. But the truth is, we never know how strong we are until to go on is the only choice we have. Throughout the day we can find courage in the wise words of a sweet little fish and quietly whisper, "*Just keep swimming. Just keep swimming.*"

Every day we are faced with a new curveball, and whether we are ready for it or are completely blindsided is on us. We need to switch to our superhero form and do what we do. Some days might be handled more gracefully than others, but what needs to be done gets done.

We watch the same television shows and movies over and over to the point where we can recite each and every line of the characters. We bounce and dance and sing to the same songs, again and again, and despite feeling as if our head might pop if we hear it one more time, we still smile and belt out singing as if this were one of our all-time favorites.

Motherhood is the perfectly imperfect job. We have the ability to take failures and messes and turn them into beautiful disasters. We have the ability to tell the doubters to step aside and watch it be done. We have the ability to turn the impossible into the possible.

As mothers, we have learned that, unfortunately, life doesn't get easier for us, but rather, we must get stronger. We make mistakes and we pray to God that we've learned from them the first time around. We scrape and search tirelessly for mental toughness, and when our bodies say no, our minds come back with a fierce *YES.*

# TO THAT FAMILY

*L*

You can see (or more likely *hear*) us coming from a mile away. You might think we're playing charades as you watch my husband and me make hand signals to each other, gritting our teeth and delivering *the* silent threat to one of the kids: *This is it. Never again!* Only it's the thousandth *never again* that we're threatening.

We do our best cleaning ten minutes before we're expecting company. And two minutes after the house is somewhat presentable, it's already back to...well, *normal.*

When we stroll into church (and on a *good* Sunday we're running only a handful of minutes late), it has been said on more than one occasion that the "entertainment" has arrived. Yep, we're *those* people.

We probably turn the dryer on about five more times than necessary to "re"-fluff the clothes that have been waiting to be folded for, wait...what day is it? People in the grocery stores, malls, amusement parks...yes, they *all* love to hate us. We're those people coming with two shopping carts, the double stroller (and trust me, nobody likes the lady taking up the aisle space pushing the double stroller), with the kids dashing and darting everywhere they probably shouldn't be.

It's safe to say we haven't slept in seven years and, more than likely, won't for at least seven more.

We barely fit in our vehicle adequately, and no matter if it's a day trip or overnight, we have to bring along twelve bags of supplies to sanely survive. But not to worry; if something should go missing, we could probably find an extra sock, a few pairs of shoes, an extra sippy cup, a pacifier, or a sweatshirt strewn throughout our vehicle in places you never even knew existed.

We have been invited to fewer and fewer places as our family gets bigger and bigger and people's tolerance for our sweet circus gets shorter and shorter.

We buy enough food and toiletries to supply a small army, but yet, somehow, within days of our shopping extravaganza paper towels, toilet paper, diapers, or wipes will undoubtedly need to be purchased again.

Mealtimes usually involve someone crying, screaming, bucking in their chair, or randomly getting out of their seat to go bust a move in the middle of the kitchen. One end of the spectrum or the other, no in between. Yep, that's how we roll, twenty-three hours a day, six and a half days a week.

You can usually find me running around the house, nursing a baby in one arm and chasing two other toddlers with my "free" hand while being beckoned by another kiddo from another part of the house. The dog is barking. Someone is knocking at the door. The phone is ringing. And the smoke alarm is going off from my attempt at cooking. You think you just read about *these* people and watch them in a movie, but, no, that's us. We're *those* people.

Our bed is about four sizes too small. And by *our* bed, I mean the *entire family's* bed, since no one likes to sleep in their own.

Snacktime is all day, every day. When we go to someone's house, you'd swear we hadn't fed our children in weeks. For being ages six and under, I'm terrified to think of feeding them as teenagers.

I'm not ashamed that I look forward to pizza night each Friday or that I love our paper plates more than any dishware we own.

We work hard, and we play hard. We fight hard, but we love even harder.

Yep, we're that family. That crazy one I envisioned for pretty much my entire life.

And to be honest, I wouldn't want it any other way.

We're crazy. We lost our minds long ago. We are deliriously exhausted... And deliriously in love.

In love with the crazy people that we get to call *our* family.

So the next time *you* get the infamous eye roll, the whispers that were meant loud enough for you to hear, or feel that your family is completely abnormal and has completely lost it, you're probably doing something right.

# TO THE ALMOST MOM OF TWO

*L*

Today I met a mom at my local bookstore who was about to have her second baby; she was an almost mom of two. My son, a kindergartner, started school a few weeks ago, and so it's just been my one-year-old daughter and me making our way through our days together. We really went because I was craving a latte, but it's also a nice place simply to sit, without feeling guilty, as there is a play area for my daughter to enjoy. When I arrived at the train table, two mothers were already there, toddlers in tow. My daughter joined their children and the kids quickly began to play together.

It was impossible not to notice that one mom was pregnant, and as I joined in the conversation, I asked when she was due with baby two. The baby was set to arrive in four weeks— right before her daughter turns two. Her excitement was obvious and contagious, and I quickly said, "Wow, that's great! Your kids will be so close." But I could sense a bit of hesitation and nervousness when she responded with, "Yeah, that's the idea. We planned it this way, but they will be *so* close in age." She asked if I had other children, and I told her that I did and that they are five years apart. We continued our conversation, lighthearted and child-centered, and after a while, my daughter and I packed up to go home. As we were leaving, I wished the pregnant mother well with her new transition. I try not to give unsolicited advice, especially to strangers, and so I didn't, but here's what I wish I had known before I became a mom of two:

**You can love another child.** I've heard this fear that you can't from many parents and I admit that I was worried, too. The love for my son seemed all-encompassing. What I've learned, though, is that love is exponential. And I've learned that while I love my children equally, it's hard to quantify. I also love them very differently. I never understood that love could feel so diverse.

**It is normal for your child to feel resentment for the younger sibling.** I didn't realize this, and despite the excitement my son had for the birth of his little sister, after about two weeks, he was ready to send her back. When she was a month old, he smacked her hand because she wouldn't stop crying. The resentment is normal, and eventually, it will all even out.

**It doesn't matter how far apart in age your kids are, there will be challenges.** I've heard many mothers talk about the ideal age gap, but I actually wonder if that exists. For example, my son is five years older than my daughter, and while that seems like it might be easier (and maybe it is!), we are starting all over again with an infant. My son has been a wonderful sleeper for much of his life, but after the baby was born, he would wake up at night, too. And then we would all be exhausted. That is just one of many challenges we faced.

**If you feel guilty, know that you're not alone.** I felt so guilty after my daughter was born. Maybe it was the hormones, but I missed all the one-on-one time I'd had with my son. I felt guilty because there were so many adjustments, and mostly, I felt like I was failing. New moms of more than one: I hope you don't feel guilty and you shouldn't. But if you do, know that you're not alone.

**Take help when it's offered.** I was lucky to have people who would take my son for an hour or so here and there so that I could focus on the baby. My daughter cried all the time and while I needed a break, my son needed it more. He would have fun with a friend and I could just bounce the baby for a few hours or hold her while she slept without feeling guilty.

**Maintain your first child's schedule.** A friend recommended this to me, but I didn't listen at first and opted to keep my son at home with me and the baby. But he needed the structure of his preschool, so after about two weeks of him being home with us, I enrolled him for the morning option. It gave him just enough time to maintain his own identity, outside of his newfound role as "big brother."

**Your relationship with your partner might go through another transition.** With the adjustment to two children, my husband and I found it harder to connect. As we navigated new family dynamics and schedules, we had to try harder to be especially kind to one another. And we fought more. That first year of being the parents of two kids was rough for us, and from what I've heard, this is pretty normal. We weathered the storm, though, and came out better connected.

**Don't compare yourself to other mothers.** I have friends who are mothers to three, four, and five kids. When I was adjusting to being a mom of two, I felt like I was failing because they seemed to be mothering with such ease. The reality is that they all have rough days, too.

**Try not to forget yourself.** If you can, take a break. Go for a walk. Run to Target. Take a bath. Read a book. It's easy to feel like you can't get away, but you need to make time to connect with yourself, too.

**Enjoy this time.** Some of the best moments in my life so far have been in the past year as I've watched my children fall in love with one another. When my children light up when they see each other, it makes all of the struggles worth it.

# FOR ALL OF MY FELLOW BUSY MOTHERS

*L*

I'm currently creating my "NOT To-Do List." Yes, you heard me correctly. And I'm probably working more diligently on this than any other list I've ever made.

Ask any successful person. Talk to the most organized person you know. Interview someone who has a perfect track record of getting things done. One thing they all have in common is their "to-do list." Research shows that it helps. It *works*. Writing something down is a step toward ensuring that you will more than likely do it.

But with all of our growing to-do lists, we have a diminishing *living* of sorts. We no longer can simply *be*. We are fearful of being judged for laziness—that taking the few moments to rest, the few minutes to enjoy, the time to *be* will be a direct correlation to our lacking a work ethic and being unmotivated, unambitious, lazy.

Pressure.

Oh, the pressures we face today.

The pressure to be the perfect mother. The perfect wife. The perfect friend. The perfect businesswoman.

Why is there not more pressure to live life to the fullest?

Why isn't it normal in our society to admire someone sitting at the park, watching their children play, without being hooked on their cell phone? That simple accomplishment deserves a medal all on its own.

We rush from one event to the next. We hurry to finish one task just to get to the next one, yet fifteen more still await us.

We go, fearing to stop because our bodies may crash and burn.

We praise the people overdoing it. We applaud the successful overworkers. And we look down upon or, worse, don't even acknowledge those who take the time to *be*.

Why don't we create a "Don't-Do List" instead, in order to indulge in the things that are most important in this world?

We are in danger of burning out.

We are human beings.

The important word is *being*.

To simply exist.

Being lost in the moment.

Being at peace with the world.

Being kinder to ourselves.

Being kinder to others.

Being able to let go and proud to do so.

I'm not saying we don't need women who are out there every single day, trying to make change ... trying to *be* the change in the world.

I'm not saying we don't need go-getters who are on a mission to capture their dreams while leaving their mark on the world.

I'm not saying we don't need doers.

But we do need more time *being*. We need more of living in the moment rather than speeding through every opportunity that will soon come to pass.

So as you indulge in success and opportunity and business, coupled with the constant battle of climbing up the ladder, remember that at the top of your list should be simply...being. Living. Breathing. Enjoying.

This very moment is the perfect teacher. Be ready to listen. Be ready to act. And yes, be ready to sometimes be called to just be.

Embrace the challenge!

# TO MAMA, MOMMY, OR MOM: THEY ALL MEAN THE SAME

$\mathcal{L}$

We are mamas or mommies or moms, but no matter what our children call us: We are their mothers forever and ever.

"There's my baby," I said, whispering into her hair as we made a flower arrangement from flowers we picked in the garden.

"Hey, Mama," was her reply and she handed me a purple lilac from her chubby little fingers with the crease in her wrist. Her hands always remind me that she's a baby, my baby, and I am still her favorite person, her mama.

My almost two-year-old daughter used these turn of words recently. And even though it's cute, the phrase seems too old for her to be saying. I was transported, sliding on her words into the future I know awaits me—a future where my baby girl is no longer a baby at all and where she goes from calling me Mama to Mom. I know how soon it will be.

She's only 22 months old, but soon, I know she'll be 22 and graduating from college. I can't help but wonder if she'll sneak up behind me and put her arms around me right before it's time for her to go on stage to get her diploma. I imagine her saying "Hey" but the "mama" will be long gone and replaced with "mom." "Hey, Mom," she will say and my heart will swell like it does now. *There's my baby*, I will think, watching her in her cap and gown, the diploma a step further along on the road to her dreams.

Her hair is a strawberry blond but seems to be darkening. It's curly and rather unruly and there is only enough of it for a short ponytail. But someday, she'll be getting ready for her senior prom, and those curls will glisten as her signature. She might not like them, even though I hope she does. I imagine her in navy because her eyes are the bluest blue, but knowing my girl, she'll wear something totally original and she won't care about matching her eyes to her dress. And I will watch her with pride as she gets her photo taken and smiles at me, her mom. "There's our baby," I will whisper to my husband.

Her brother is five years older and I watch how she desperately tries to keep up. She follows him everywhere, saying "bro bro." He once called me "mama," but now only calls me "mom" and before long, she'll follow in his footsteps like every other time. He's the first one she asks for in the morning and the last one she kisses at night. Tonight, he went to spend the night with my parents, and she said to him, "Stay here," as she blocked the door. And I can't help but feel her heartache when he leaves our nest five years before her to set sail into the world. But I will be there to greet her in the morning and kiss her before she goes to bed. And while one baby boy will be gone on his own adventure, I will kiss her forehead and say to her, "There's my baby," as a way to reassure her that it will all be okay. It might annoy her but I will say it anyway because she'll always be my baby.

She threw a fit today, throwing herself down in a rage. It was raining in sheets and she wanted to be outside. I tried to tell her that we would go when the rain slowed, but she wouldn't listen. And, I can see her slamming her door in high school, upset for another decision I've made in her best interest. While the fits and frustrations of toddlerhood will be over eventually, raising a teenager won't be easy, no matter how it all goes. Even though raising such a strong-willed child can be trying, most times I admire her resolution. Even in those times, as I know I will fight back my own feelings of frustration, I also know I will still admire her independence and think to myself, *There's my baby.*

"There's my baby," I said again after I thanked her for the gift of my favorite flower.

"There, Mama," she replied and hugged me.

Friends, here we are. Frustrations and tantrums, hairstyles and proms, graduations and departures, and everything in between. The good, the bad, and the ugly. But more beauty than all else.

Yes. Here is mama or mommy or mom. Always.

# TO EVERY MOTHER WHO HAS GONE CRAZY

*L*

My kids drive me crazy. Does that make me a bad parent? About to have my fourth baby, I realize that it took me years to find the courage to say it out loud, but they do...They can drive me mad. And the grueling schedule of Mommy-duty 24 hours a day, 365 days a year can be, well...I need a new word for "exhausting."

Haul one load of laundry down the stairs. Empty the basket into the wash. Start the cycle. Fold the laundry in the dryer. Take the empty basket back into the bathroom to find piles of dirty clothes and towels already strewn everywhere, enough for another load ready to go.

Breakfast. Clean up. Snacktime. Clean up. Lunchtime. Clean up. Dinnertime. Clean up. Snack before bed. Clean up. It's safe to say you could stay in the kitchen all day, morning, noon, and night, preparing and serving and cleaning up. It's an entire job, all on its own.

I sweep the floors after each meal, and despite doing this multiple times a day, you'd think our floor hasn't been touched in months. It almost makes me gag a bit, at the sight of exactly what I sweep up, again, just hours after it was already done.

To be able to find a matching pair of shoes is a true task in itself. Everywhere I go, I'm tripping or swimming past a sea of shoes. Naturally, never with its pair, a random shoe or sock (okay, who am I kidding...or sippy cup or spoon) might be mixed in with toys, strewn clothes, or random items that need to be tossed or organized. The closet designated just for shoes is overflowing to the point that there are days I'm tempted to just throw them all out.

Dishes. The dishwasher is running. Both sides of the sink are beginning to fill up even while little hands reach over the counter to throw in another dirty sippy cup or plate. Nothing is impossible, however, but to ever really be fully caught up on the dishes, just as the laundry goes, is, it is safe to say...impossible.

One baby needs a diaper change, the other toddler is screaming that they need to be wiped on the potty, while another is hollering from a different floor in the house that you need to come quick, *It's an emergency.*

I'm pretty certain we keep our hardworking garbagemen in business. I don't know how so much can accumulate in so little time. Each of the designated trash cans fills up. Out they go. A new bag goes in as another is ready to be emptied. I wish we could trade in and recycle diapers, tissues, and wipes because by this point, I'd easily be a millionaire.

The vacuum gets run through the main rooms daily. This, too, doesn't seem to make a difference as I hear it click and crunch over the carpet's surface. And when I empty it, I can't believe I just let my children crawl over what was beneath them.

It's comforting to know that if we ever got stranded some-where, we'd have a full survival pack of...well, just about anything and everything in our vehicle. This is often where one of the random missing socks or shoes turns up, along with the missing sweatshirt that was tucked under a seat for some time and the pacifier that was lodged between the seats in the back row. With the constant rushing from work to practices to games to events to appointments, it is a race to and from the car. And whatever is left behind will more than likely be found within the next couple of months when we find the ten extra minutes to clean the thing out.

If it's 6:02 a.m. on a Saturday morning, and if we're just *now* hearing noise or tiny feet running to our room, then I guess we should be grateful. Sleep is for the weak, right?

Have to go to the bathroom? When you do *finally* make it there, just be prepared to have company, or, if you are bold enough to lock the door, prepare yourself to have tiny people trying to bang the door down or stick their hands underneath it in the hope that they will be able to reach you.

Some neighbors must think we hold either rock concerts or WWE wrestling matches in our house. Depending upon the time of day and the mood of the kids, there could be screaming and all-out battles between our toddlers. Someone is always yelling, "Mommy!" *every* minute of *every* hour of *every* single day. There are days you feel enslaved in your own home when not a second is ever found to be your own.

And then I stop to think...

If I didn't have the never-ending laundry, that means I

wouldn't have little arms around my neck to help balance themselves as I put their pants on or would never get those kisses on my nose or the sweetest stares as we are forehead to forehead, even if it is the seventh time I'm redressing them for the day.

If I weren't tripping over tiny little shoes and picking up mismatched socks, I wouldn't have precious feet to hold and kiss and tickle and massage every single day.

If I didn't have dishes to do and meals to serve, I would have a large, empty dining room table and a boring, lifeless atmosphere without the unpredictable, charming, and unfailing livelihood that encompasses it several times each day. Yes, a quiet, cleaner kitchen; however, not one full of memories, no matter how messy they may be.

If I wasn't awakened before sunrise, I wouldn't have a reason to climb out of bed each morning and meet the new day's adventures that await me. The little monkeys that rule, terrorize, and run in every direction are my very reason to carry on.

If I didn't have the constant commotion and noise, the silence would be nearly deafening. I remember from such an early age that I yearned for a big family of my *own*. And with a big family comes big love, big noise, and yes, lots of commotion. Commotion that is also filled with an abundant amount of such genuine joy that nothing else on earth could equally fill me.

So...if I wasn't *needed*, to put it simply...I'd be lost.

Some days, no, correction...*every day* is an energy-draining, roller coaster of a marathon that I just bravely attempt to keep up with. However, it's one wild, demanding, rewarding ride that I can't picture a day without.

Yes, my kids drive me crazy. It took me so long to be able to bravely say that out loud for fear that it meant I was a terrible mother. But it's the crazy circus full of laughter and love that I've dreamed about and prayed for my entire life. These little people are the absolute loves of my life.

So the next time you're ready to pull your hair out, do two things: Remember that you are *not* alone. And then sit back, laugh, and enjoy. This is one hell of a ride that you're on. And it will be over before you know it.

Turn the music on, pick up a child, and dance, love, laugh, and just **be** in these moments with them. There's *nothing* that a little love and laughter can't heal or touch.

# TO A FELLOW KINDERGARTEN MOM

## *L*

I met you today at kindergarten orientation. The boys were both tentative, but my son came up to yours and asked his name. Your son was quiet but warmed up to mine right away. After a few minutes, they ran to the corner of the classroom to play with a few toys. I could see your face relax as I felt my shoulders fall. The pain in my back reminded me that I had been tensing my own shoulders since I walked in the door. We were both relieved that they had found one another and we mentioned how each boy was nervous coming into the orientation. And, we told one another how we were both nervous as first-time kindergarten moms.

Just this morning, I looked at him and noticed that his cheeks are going away. That might sound so weird, but everyone, everywhere, has always commented on his chubby cheeks. Maybe I didn't even notice them because lately, people haven't been commenting on them as much. His face is now thinning out, taking on the earliest shape of the young man I will come to know. It's just a hint of what he will look like, but the baby cheeks he's had seem to be going. His smile now takes up the largest part of his face, electric, contagious. Instead of his cheeks, that radiant smile is now his signature.

His shorts are suddenly too short, as his legs seem to understand that he's about to start kindergarten. We measured him and he's grown two inches since the start of the summer. I looked at him this morning and I teared up because he seemed to shift, right there before my eyes, from a baby to a little boy ready to start a new chapter. I'm sure you're noticing these things, too...

In the middle of orientation, my son came up to me and crawled into my lap. I was surprised, really, because he seldom does this unless we are at home—he hasn't crawled into my lap in front of others for a while now. I drew him close and held him, and I listened as he told me that he had been nervous but he was happy he'd made a friend so quickly. I looked around the room and saw your son with his arms around your leg. They might be starting kindergarten, but they are still our babies, you know? We are opening our arms and sharing them with the world, but they are still our little boys. I think they will always be our babies, in one way or another.

After I put my son to bed, I went through old pictures and found one of me on my first day of kindergarten in 1984. I had on a crocheted white poncho and was standing in front of the school bus. It's a total throwback picture—the yellowed camera paper from thirty-one years ago. Believe it or not, I looked a lot like my son does now—I can see his face in mine. I remember that day well. I was lucky to have my brother and sister on that bus with me; I took comfort in sitting with my big brother. He held my hand on the entire ride—the entire thirty minutes on back roads to get to our rural school—and when we finally got there, he walked me into the classroom. I remember seeing him in the hallway later and he smiled at me. I felt safe and loved, even though I was very scared. Like me, I'm sure you're replaying your first day of kindergarten as you get your little son's backpack ready and buy his new school clothes.

*"We're in this together,"* I said as we parted ways, and I meant it. Little girls who started kindergarten over thirty years ago, in separate schools, in separate areas, now have little boys starting kindergarten together in this same school, in this same area. And you know what, Mama? We *can* do this together. Let's walk back to our cars together. I have chocolate in case you need it.

*L*

I remember our walk into the hospital. He had one hand in front of my stomach and one behind my back, to brace me, just in case I would forget how to put one foot in front of the other and stumble. I was only a few weeks along and we were heading to get blood work done to verify the pregnancy. And despite my giggling and playfully pushing him away since I was more than fine, it was one of the most endearing things for me to recall to this day, him trying his best to put the baby and me in a bubble to protect us from any remote danger that could potentially come.

He would cook almost every dinner, do the cleanups, and make sure I took my daily nap every night after work. I appreciated and enjoyed (and at the time felt I *needed* all of this) his caretaking as my body adjusted to the exhaustion of growing another human being. At this point, taking care of ourselves and our dog was a full-time job in itself, so I decided to take full advantage of any pampering and extra rest I could sneak in.

For my second pregnancy, I thought that I must be Superwoman. Now I was taking care of a husband, two dogs, a two-year-old, teaching twenty little children each day, and oh, yes, growing another human being. My energy level seemed to diminish on a daily basis and in between my lovely side effects of the pregnancy, which included migraines and morning sickness (which should change its name to *all-day* sickness). I thought there was no way I would survive some of those days.

My husband and I were still getting used to our busy lives with just one toddler and normally "tag-teamed" to help things run smoothly. Occasionally, I would be able to sneak in a nap when the baby did, but for the most part, this pregnancy did not mirror my first *at all*. The extra attention went to our daughter, which I wouldn't have wanted any other way, but I realized that the days of coddling the woman who was carrying the baby were over.

Just when we figured out how to divide and conquer and play man-to-man defense, things got crazier. While one of us would sprint after a toddler running one way, the other had to dash in the complete opposite direction. And then, yep, you guessed it, I got pregnant with our third. And without a doubt, I thought I was losing my mind at times.

Still keeping up with the regimen of the house, a husband, two toddlers, two dogs, and twenty students every day while being pregnant was typical; however, we decided to make things even more exciting. As our family continued to grow, our home and living space continued to shrink. So we decided that we needed a bigger house. Now I was not only dealing with a zoo, but trying to pack up an entire house while painting and organizing and setting up our new one.

I'm not sure if one nap ever took place, and as far as

managing to get my feet up, that happened only when I collapsed into someone's bed or randomly took a nap on one of the babies' floors. At this point, as I carried another massive baby in my belly, I had one toddler on one of my hips, one wrapped around my leg, and a moving box in my *free* arm. My husband and I were just blown away on a daily basis that we all survived another day's adventures.

Going from two to three naturally added to the circus. However, in some respects, we had become experts at managing madness. When I was having a nervous breakdown, my husband held us all up; and when he was breaking down, thankfully, I was on strong and steady ground. Some days it was all we could do to keep everyone safe and sound until bedtime, while other days ran almost effortlessly. But just as we'd gotten some of the waves calmed, there we were . . . with number four scheduled to arrive at the end of the summer.

This pregnancy has been by far the most draining on my body for mainly the obvious reason of keeping up with my schedule and now three little people. I had a baby at 24, 26, 28, and now will at 30, and, naturally, the years have almost seemed to multiply in taking a greater toll on my body. Every day I'm trying to keep up with the greatest miracle, the most unfathomable mystery, the most amazing wonder— pregnancy. As I struggle through each day with the numerous burdens that creep up on me, at some point, I'm slapped in the face with a glaring reminder that the blessings, by far, outweigh the encumbrances.

Simply because of what our daily life *demands*, I no longer get the pampering and attention I did when we were pregnant with our first child. My days don't consist of mentally or physically relaxing and finding tranquil moments to prepare myself for this monumental experience that is nearly upon us. Rather, they're filled with quite the opposite, but I am humbled to think that soon enough I'll be surrounded by four tiny people, four miracles, that *I* brought into this world.

My best days begin and end with a child snuggled into some side or part of me. I think it's a proven fact that no matter how many babies keep coming, they all find *their* spot on or around Mommy. And the most astounding fact of all is, despite what the job calls for, there is always enough of Mommy to go around. Certainly there are moments and days when it seems that is the furthest thing from the truth, but somehow, someway, there always is.

And that, right there, is why we're simply incredible. We **do** the unthinkable. We **conquer** the impossible. We **prove** on a daily basis to be extraordinary. We go by the name of **Mom**.

And if we're lucky enough to find a partner to hold on to as we try to do better than survive this amazingly crazy ride, well...life is good.

III.

An entire decade.

After celebrating my fourth baby's first birthday, I have come to realize that by the time I am done breast-feeding her, I will have been pregnant and/or nursing for almost a decade.

Wow.

For one third of my life my body has not been my own. I have been creating, housing, nurturing, reproducing, providing, sharing, I guess basically...*living* and *breathing* with and *for* someone else.

Pregnancy time alone, four years. Yes, almost four years of sharing my body, carrying another human being around that was growing within me, and

- 40 months of gaining weight, growing in places I never knew could grow, and my body forever...well, *changing* (the most polite word for all of the shapes moving, body parts shifting, and areas sagging, inflating, deflating, and reinflating over and over again);
- 160 weeks of intermittent nausea, vomiting, migraines, and shooting back pain. Need I say more?
- 1,120 days of hormonal changes, mood swings, and

laughing and sobbing hysterically...at the same time; and

- 26,880 hours of ongoing back pain (well, full body pain and spasms), sleep insomnia, and severe exhaustion.
- And lo and behold, each pregnancy transitioned right up to labor. *Oh, the labor:*
- 3 days of withstanding pain that the human body somehow is able to endure, while, by the pure grace of God, not shutting down;
- 36 hours of preparing to push a human being out of me. Truly laboring, about to do something that is the most natural thing in this earth, yet takes the most inhuman, supernatural strength;
- 2,160 minutes of working and breathing my way through each contraction. And by contraction, I mean that feeling as if someone were taking a knife and stabbing me over and over again in my stomach. And as soon as I was able to regroup and catch my breath, sure enough, another minute, another contraction would follow;
- My God, the female body is simply *incredible.*
- And each delivery led straight into time spent nursing.
- 2,678,400 minutes of tirelessly feeding, pulling, squeezing, yanking, and, yes, sometimes even pain and discomfort.
- 44,640 hours of producing milk, my body physically creating the healthiest, most nutritional meal possible, filled with antibodies that only I can give my babies. (Wow, I wonder if they need a new Superwoman cartoon persona...I could always throw my name in for the running, yes?)

- 1,860 days of waking each night, all night, sometimes hourly, and often multiple times an hour to feed, to console, to quench my babies' hunger. (And if my Superwoman gig didn't pan out, I could always use my stamina for a Duracell battery commercial and run beside that little drummer bunny that just keeps going…and going…and going…)
- 5 years of my body providing nutrients, actual meals for my children. Yep, Betty Crocker ain't got nothing on this mama. Speaking of Betty Crocker, I have provided my babies 2,610 meals every year; 13,050 meals total; 104,400 ounces of milk.
- 248 weeks of on-and-off pumping, breast-feeding, feeling engorged, then rushing off to pump in my short allotted time at work.
- 62 months of constantly being on call and ready to be the "milkwoman"…any time, any place. But when I was called to duty, I showed up to the plate every time.
- And then we move into the territory of sleep. Or…the lack thereof.
- 8½ years of not having one, not a single, blessed, full night of rested, uninterrupted sleep.
- 3,102 days of going to bed late (and "going to bed" includes collapsing in any bed or on any floor) or waking up early (and somehow managing to keep my eyes pried open to ensure the children stay alive).
- 74,448 hours of functioning with severe sleep deprivation, performing one of the hardest, most daunting, selfless jobs on the planet, trying to survive in the world we call parenthood.

- 4,466,000 minutes of having bags under my eyes, praying that tonight the baby will just sleep through the night. And if that prayer should be answered, that only means a toddler will be up crying from a bad dream, someone will wet the bed or start puking. Yes, it's just...hmmm, life as we know it. Who really needs sleep anyway?

So, to accurately sum things up, I'm pretty tired. Okay, I'm flipping exhausted, out of my mind, lost my sanity (hell, lost my pride) several years ago. And at this point, I can safely say that things aren't going back to normal anytime soon.

But. (There's always the infamous *but*...)

This physically exhausted body has accomplished and performed miracles. It's done the unthinkable. I can say I've created life, given birth to life, and then was given the privilege of sustaining life.

And at the end of each day, when all of my children are healthy and safe, I can collapse somewhere and praise God that we all made it through another day.

But the next time I complain or get down on myself and become discouraged about what I can't do or might not be able to do as well or as fast anymore, I need to remind myself that this body (no matter what it looks like or what has changed) has accomplished wonders.

I will have given a decade of myself over to four tiny humans.

And it's probably safe to say that this decade has been, is, and will remain the most self-sacrificing, exhausting, mind-boggling, fulfilling, rewarding, and empowering time of my life.

# A NOTE ABOUT THE FIRST CRUSH

*L*

We recently went to our first parent-teacher association meeting in my son's new school and I discovered that he has a crush. He's just finished his first marking period of kindergarten, and because we had no babysitter, we took both kids to the meeting with us. We arrived just on time and joined the other parents in the small gymnasium. The meeting began and my daughter, too busy and loud to stay, was ushered to the playground by my husband. My son normally would follow my husband outside at the chance to play, but he didn't that night. He asked if he could stay inside with me. I was confused at first because I couldn't imagine why he would opt to stay inside at a "boring meeting," but then I realized the reason for his request: an adorable little girl with sea-foam green eyes and honey-colored hair.

As I listened intently to the words of his principal, I occasionally turned around to see my son with this little girl. We have many friends with daughters and he plays with them all the time; however, there was something different in his interactions with this girl with the green eyes. There was a twinkle in his eye, a sly smile on his face. I watched them play rock, paper, scissors—just like I did so many years ago. It was just the two of them, playing and talking. I kept my focus on the words of the principal, only to hear a snicker and turn to see this girl, smaller than my son, with her arms around him in a jacketed position. He could have easily gotten out of this embrace, but he was smiling and I just smiled back, raising an eyebrow. The little girl smiled, too.

After the meeting, I asked my son about his relatively new friend. He told me how much he liked her and how he felt differently about her; he liked her in a way he hadn't liked someone before. I kept the conversation casual, of course, but I couldn't help asking what he liked about her most. He said, "Well, liking her is just an experience." His face flickered as he held back a smile. He was quiet for a second and I was going to move onto another topic, but then he said, "Actually, I like her because she is kind and smart." His face lit up as he told me about her, and for the first time, I saw my son in a new light—the light of a little boy, smitten by a fellow kindergartner, his very first crush.

Later, as I thought about this little girl, I realized he had said nothing to me at all about what she looked like. He didn't comment on how her hair color is like wheat or that her eyes are like the color of the ocean as it meets the shore. He said nothing about her mismatched clothing, which I admired because it showed her strong sense of self; I could tell she picked her own clothes and I liked her for it. He simply told me how she was kind and smart, and that's all that mattered to him. At six, he sees her for who she is. I hope he always looks through those eyes.

He rattled on about her for a bit and then our conversation ended. But not before I told him that I thought those were great reasons to like a person, and how, actually, those were the reasons I liked many of the people in my life. Someday, even though it seems like it will be so far away, I'm sure, or at least I hope, we will have more serious conversations about school, friends, his dreams, and, of course, the crushes he has and even the first time he falls in love. And I will be sure to listen, just like I did today.

His confession reminded me that day to be sure I'm listening him always, because I want him to keep sharing. And for now, this crush on his fellow kindergarten classmate is so important to him. He also called me to look beyond the surface to the soul of people. My son sees his little friend's soul, and he admires her for genuine reasons. What more could any of us ask for from the people who love us? To look them in the eye and see their soul? We just want them to see us as a child does. And in some ways, that's love at its purest. How often do we look at others and see them for what they look like or what they have or do? How amazing would it be to see people with childlike wonder?

For now, he's still my little boy who has a crush on a little girl, and I'm so happy he told me about it.

# TO MY HOPEFUL MOTHER

*L*

There are so many pros to having your babies close together. They always have a playmate. You never feel like you have to start over with the entire process because you're already in it. You become pretty fabulous at juggling twenty balls in the air at one time and are ready for pretty much anything that can be thrown at you. Literally.

You go through sleep deprivation all at once, night after night, month after month, year after year. You don't even notice the bags under your eyes anymore as they have permanently taken up residence and now just seem to . . . fit.

And you've become accustomed to chaos every second of every minute of every day. So accustomed that you don't even realize the circus you are putting on for everyone in public, because if you did, more than likely you'd join them and roll your eyes at yourself, too, as antic after antic continues.

But I, for one, happen to love my three-ring spectacle. My daily life craziness is actually the normal that I prayed for my entire life. Frankly, I wouldn't trade it for the most quiet, organized, successful, well-traveled, well-rested lifestyle. But that is just me. And for those of you silently asking yourself if I'm crazy and have totally lost it, the answer is *yes . . . a long time ago!*

But when you have a crew like mine and you venture out in public, people have the opportunity to do one of two things: They either fall in love with you and show that they adore your beautiful, entertaining monkeys by ooohing and awwwing and chuckling at the tricks of your littler performers; or they absolutely, positively despise you and are irritated by everything about your entire crew, including each move and every noise.

But one would think you'd at least get some slack from other parents who are going through or have gone through the same things. Right? That they'd get it? They don't hate you for being the one hogging grocery aisles with three shopping carts and three crying children, or, heaven forbid, taking up three times the space on a sidewalk or one side of the mall or fairground with the double stroller. Yes, being the woman pushing the stroller—oh, the looks could kill.

But the other parents are supposed to be on the same team. Battling the same battles. Fighting the same fights. Holding on while they ride the same roller coaster you're currently being flung around on; knuckles white from holding on so tightly for dear life.

But, as with anything, you have your Negative Nancys and Debbie Downers. And unfortunately, they are everywhere. At the grocery store, at church, at the park, at the mall, at the gas station, and, sadly, they even find you out of town visiting family and friends. They're everywhere. And the best part is, they manage to sneak up on you with their words of wisdom at the most inopportune times.

The baby is bucking in the grocery cart, but you must keep pushing through despite what the best parenting research says: Show your child that you won't put up with that behavior in public and leave immediately. Well, I apologize to everyone in Walmart, but I, for one, cannot leave and must get my groceries. It's now or never. And before my trip is over, at least one or two other shoppers lean over and share as if they're actually helping, *"Oh, you just wait. It gets worse."*

My toddler is speaking out in the middle of church. Okay, he's yelling. We do what we can, take him out to the cry area, use as many quieting techniques as possible. Just then the older woman behind us whispers, *"It's okay, dear. Don't worry. Mine went through that stage. He'll grow out of it. But boy, hold on. You'll have so many other issues to deal with when this phase fizzles out. You'll be wishing you had this back."*

It's a beautiful, sunny day and the kids are running around and laughing at the park. Everyone seems to be having a great time until the baby falls on the cement from running ahead too fast and busts open her knee. A bystander pipes in, *"Oh, poor thing. You always hate to see them get hurt. In a handful of years you'll be afraid to let them leave the house and have to worry about each time they get in the car with one of their friends or go out on a date. Ugh, I wish these were the booboos I still had to worry about fixing. Just wait. It gets worse!"*

All three kids are shrieking and running underneath the clothes racks in a store at the mall. Everyone in the store seems to be quite annoyed, as if we are purposefully trying to ruin their relaxing day out. Another dad walks by and says out the side of his mouth, *"You think things are tough now? Ha! You have no idea! It only gets worse."*

The kids are fighting and hitting each other in the backseat of the car while we're filling up at the gas station. The person across from us chuckles as they're being entertained by the impromptu WWE show going on in the back of our vehicle and says, *"Reminds me of how mine used to be. They still hate each other to this day, and they're all in their mid- to late teens now. I hope one day they'll get along."*

You're at home for the holidays and run into friends of the family who haven't seen you in a couple of years. You have the kids dressed in their best and are ecstatic to show off your picture-perfect, beautiful, intelligent, personable, glowing children. Naturally, as soon as they are approached and asked their name or how old they are, they shut down, stick their faces into your leg, and shake their heads back and forth while screaming *"NO!"* The family friends are quick to respond, *"Oh, it's okay. I'm sure they're trying to adjust from being out of their normal routine and away from home. Try to enjoy this time since they grow up so fast; before you know it, they'll want nothing to do with you. My kids never want to talk or be around me. Soon you won't have this."*

When we get these comments, normally I do the infamous smile and the happiest fake giggle I can force out and reply with something like, *"Oh, I can only imagine!"* Or nervously laugh and say, *"They're something else, aren't they?"* But most of the time I want to look them square in the eyes and ask, *"Really? Thanks a million for the great pep talk! Now I feel so much better! Whew, that's a load off!"*

It's tough being a parent for all of us. There are different worries I'll endure and battles I'm sure to face, but I'm a mother—it's my job to worry. There will never be another day for the rest of my life that I'm not worried about my children.

As parents, we are going to encounter many defeats, but we must never be defeated. Why? The answer is simple: We're gladiators.

I leave you with this thought to ponder: **Positive thinking leads to positive outcomes.** Be that start or that bridge for the next struggling mama you encounter. A couple of words of encouragement could be a total game changer for her.

## TO THE MOTHER BEING QUESTIONED FOR HAVING *ANOTHER* BABY

*L*

We recently announced to family, friends, and coworkers that we are expecting our fourth child.

However, not everyone shared in our joy:

*"Don't you two have anything else to do?"*

*"Wait, how many kids do you have at home already?"*

*"Can you guys even afford another one?"*

*"This couldn't have been planned, right?"*

*"Wow, a fourth. Did you even want another kid?"*

Still, whatever the reasoning, the criticism didn't catch us completely off-guard. In fact, it was something we had grown accustomed to over the years with each new addition to our family.

The day we announced our first pregnancy, people were shocked. We were too young. We couldn't afford a baby. We were foolish and should have waited.

We seemed to get a pass on our second child under the guise of it "made sense" to give our daughter a sibling to play with.

We would not be so lucky with our third pregnancy. It seemed that people in my life just couldn't wrap their heads around the idea of three children and two parents all coexisting in the same home. Is it really that mind-boggling to society?

As long as we were done, then maybe we could reclaim some normalcy to our family and be responsible, stop having children, and try to deal with the chaos we already had on our hands.

But that was not in our plans.

The day after I delivered our third, I was scheduled for a tubal. My husband and I had this responsible plan laid out for months prior to my delivery. But when that day came, I burst into tears and refused to consent to the surgery. The thought that I had even agreed to this plan in the first place made me ill. My husband tried to calm me and reassured me that it was "the hormones talking" and to trust what we had decided months ago. That day, as I held my third baby in my arms, I knew right then and there that there would be a fourth. It's incredible what our maternal instincts can speak to us if we pay close attention.

And here we are, a year and a half later, a third of the way into our fourth pregnancy. And with that brings the list of questions that are asked by everyone, including ourselves at times.

How could someone possibly want to add a sixth member to their family? A fourth baby in six years; have we gone mad? Our house is already beyond chaotic, our bank account runs extremely low, and there are days we search for our sanity, and as hard as we search, it can't be found—anywhere.

Another couple of years of giving my body over. Nine

months of carrying this child to term, endless days and nights of discomfort. Another pregnancy of severe sickness, constant fatigue, and more migraines than I can count. Once again my hormones will leave me feeling as if I'm ready to jump out of my own skin at times, let alone the up-and-down roller coaster of emotions my poor family has to deal with. And after this newest member of the family enters the world, I will no longer be a home for him or her, but I will be their only source of life-giving nutrients.

I have found myself nervous, revisiting the nights I realized I was hallucinating from not getting enough sleep for not only days, weeks, or months, but rather years.

I wonder how I'll survive because some days, I have found myself completely frustrated over numerous things that are completely out of my control, but that must be endured and pushed through. Will this new addition decrease that?

We had a clear vision of light at the end of the tunnel that has now disappeared. Now we are in for a few more years of buying and changing diapers. We'll have another toddler to eventually potty train. More sleepless nights and long days of consoling this little unknowing angel through the torments of teething.

Patience and time. Two things that seem to drastically decrease in my days. My husband and three other children yearn for so much more of me; how could I find room for one more? I remember falling in love so heavily with each child, I was certain with each subsequent pregnancy I would not be able to find enough love to give to another.

There are days I find myself amazed as I handle certain situations with an evolving grace and patience. And then, more often, there are other days I find myself a mad woman, running about at 65 mph. No one is listening to me, whatever I have managed to accomplish needs to be done again, and I feel as if I'm about to break.

I go through each pregnancy trying to hold tightly to my faith. I try to chase away anxiety and fear with patience and prayer, and I tell myself time and time again that all of my complaining and worrying will do nothing but make matters worse. I read about tragic stories of complications during pregnancies and childbirth and the hardships that all too many babies come into this world facing.

There are already times in this pregnancy when I feel run down, sick, and overcome with the most intense rush of hormones. As the tears fall, I ask myself: *How in the world will I handle four?*

So... why another baby?

Considering all of this, it's still quite simple for me. I couldn't imagine having it any other way. I get to experience, for a fourth time, what some women don't get to experience at all.

When I think of bringing another baby into the world, I'm completely overcome with awe that once again, I get to experience one of the most remarkable, most intense and painful yet exhilarating, phenomena that exist on this earth: giving birth to a child.

I find consolation in my children when not one other single

person in the world understands me. You never know true peace and the best kind of heartache until your toddler wipes away one of your tears, rubs your head, and looks deep into your eyes with the most warm, sympathetic, genuine gaze that any human being is capable of giving.

I refuel myself in the most incredible way possible after hours of pacing with an inconsolable baby. When your baby finally falls fast asleep, laid perfectly against your chest as your hearts are now as one, their most perfect, tiny breath whispers in your ear. Right then and there, you wish you could hold on to this moment for longer than forever. You find yourself so still, not only for fear of waking this angel, but for fear of losing this moment.

Given the choice, would I choose another baby over a larger bank account? I'd pick a baby any day. Would I prefer to call myself rich in regard to growing numbers in my savings, or in terms of my precious, growing family? The latter has been the easiest decision of my life.

There are times where I get a short break to myself, or when the kids are finally tucked in bed for the night, and the silence can be almost deafening. I certainly appreciate peaceful, sleeping babies, yet I know there will come a time years down the road when our children will be off on their own, no longer in our home. To be able to prolong that timeline puts me at great ease.

God willing, one day our children will bless us with grandchildren. This thought leaves me feeling completely fulfilled with the utmost satisfaction. Big family, big holidays, big love . . . it truly may be one of the best gifts you could receive in this lifetime.

Family, no matter what the size, is the most important thing you will ever have in this world. If only society could see babies as they are: blessings. Oh, the battles and hardships and stressors that lie ahead, this I will not deny. But the abundant blessings that these miracles already have and will continue to bring into my life are truly immeasurable.

So here we are, another baby. Another body to clothe. Another tummy to feed. Another eighteen years of growing expenses, which then turn into car payments, college costs, and weddings.

And let me tell you: I could not be happier.

# DEAR PERFECT WIFE AND MOTHER

*L*

So many of us strive for perfection. I believe that for many of us, it's an innate desire, whether we'd like to admit it or not. After all, we are made in His image. As contradictory as it may sound, God's power is certainly made perfect in our weaknesses.

I am proud to say that I am the perfect mother. I have a perfect husband who is, likewise, a perfect father. We have a perfect marriage. So naturally, we have perfect children and a perfect family.

Before you pass a quick judgment on me, let me explain further.

*Perfect* can be defined as "having all the required or desirable elements, qualities, or characteristics; as good as it is possible to be. Absolute, complete."

Why am I a *perfect mother*? I'm perfect because in the six years that I have been blessed to hold this title, I have failed again and again and again. I have made more mistakes than I could possibly tally to this day. I have been irritable and impatient due to exhaustion and weariness. I have seen sides of myself that need much correction, that leave me feeling humbled.

But with that said, as many times as I have failed, I have gotten right back up. I have dusted myself off, looked into my eyes in the mirror, and prayed to God that each of those falls will make me a better mother. I have turned my life, my heart, my complete existence over to the constant thought of each and every decision I make and its effect on my children, our family. I never knew I was capable of the immense love I could hold until the day they placed my daughter on my chest. It was possibly the most overwhelming moment of my life. Right then and there, I was forever changed.

I know that despite the number of mistakes I've made and the mistakes I'm bound to make in the future, my love as a mother is perfect. My love for my children isn't capable of ever faltering or, for that matter, ever diminishing. My love for my children is never-ending and has no flaws to be found within it. A mother's love for her children, without argument, is perfect.

Why is my husband a *perfect father*? He changes diapers. He does the dishes. He gives the babies their baths. He brushes teeth and combs hair. He dresses kids in the morning and gets their jammies on them in the evening. He ties and reties shoelaces. He cooks meals. He rubs heads to sleep. He sleeps on hardwood floors beside toddler beds just in case the scary monster comes back. He watches *Dora*, *The Bubble Guppies*, and *Team Umizoomi* more times than any adult should. Basically, when he is not at work, he is in Daddy mode, 24 hours a day, 365 days a year (okay, maybe with the exception of NFL Draft Day and Sundays during football season).

Should he do a lot of those things? Sure. Does he want to do a lot of those things, day in and day out, even when he's sick or sleep-deprived? No. But... he does them anyway. And the majority of the time, he does them without complaint. He gives his family everything he can, but mainly he gives us *himself.*

My husband would walk across fire to the ends of the earth for our children, without hesitation. Yes, he is the perfect father.

Why is my *marriage* perfect? Our marriage has been put to the test more times than I can count. And I am no fool to believe that it's not done being tested. Throughout these tests, there have been numerous times it would have been easier to give up, to give in, and, well, call it a day. There have been hundreds of times in the past decade that my husband and I have pulled ourselves out of ruts so deep, it was hard to even imagine a light at the end of the tunnel. We've fought hard, but, thankfully, we've loved even harder. Most days I drive him absolutely nuts, and he can agitate me like no other, but I can't picture a day beginning or ending without him.

To know he loves me completely, flaws and all, may be one of the most comforting feelings in this world. He loves me as much as he knows how to love. And for that, I very well may be one of the luckiest women on this planet.

Yes, our marriage is perfect because our love has outlasted and overcome what the world says it shouldn't and very well couldn't. Our love for one another is indeed *perfect.*

Why are our *children* perfect? My children fight (okay, they battle one another), they throw temper tantrums, they complain about things they shouldn't, and every day they need more than one (or two) gentle reminders of things they should have handled correctly the first time. However, their resiliency and innocent love are captivating. Their sincere empathy, in my opinion, is why this world is still here, still continuing on. I'm not sure at what point in our childhood, teens, or adulthood we lose the ability to express that kind of love, forgiveness, endurance, and, ultimately, childlike faith.

My children... they're human. They make mistakes. But... yes, they are their own perfection. When I look into the eyes of each of them, I could get lost in their ultimate love and endless wonder that I pray to God every day they never lose. I encourage my son and daughters to be big dreamers. To think the impossible. To go after the impossible. I know that if I teach them to believe enough in themselves and never lose that, they will be able to accomplish anything in this world.

And finally, why is our *family* perfect? I have thanked and praised God every day that He had our plan, our perfect plan, laid out so carefully, so divinely, that no matter what this world has thrown at us or will continue to battle our family with, we will stand strong. We will stand together, and not if, but *when* we are brought to our knees again, we will turn and wait patiently once again, for the One who has turned each and every hardship and battle into a magnificent blessing.

So, as you can see by now, your definition of *perfect* and my definition of *perfect* may differ slightly. I am so gratified that I have found the perfection I prayed for since I was a little girl. I'm grateful that each day as I slip and make mistakes, I'm reminded in some fashion of who I want to be, what I want to create, and what my purpose is while on this earth.

Find *your* perfect. Strive for *your* perfection.

Will I ever reach the world's standards of perfection as a mother and wife? No. Will my husband ever reach the world's standards for perfection as a father or husband? Nope. Will our marriage and family and children meet those worldly standards for perfection? It's safe to say no.

But I can say one thing: I wouldn't trade *our* perfect for any other perfect in this life.

# TO THE MOM IN TARGET

*L*

Please tell me you've been that mom.

I had to make an emergency evacuation from Target. I made an egregious error and brought this little mischief-maker with me to do some Easter shopping.

My first mistake? We got into Target and she said, "This way," and pointed to the food court. I heeded her demands and turned my cart. She was sitting and smiling sweetly.

My second mistake? She asked for popcorn. I knew it was a horrible idea. I tried to convince her to get a cookie or even a slushie. But this girl is determined. And she was so cute saying "popcorn"—a word I didn't even know she knew. I fell for it, hook, line, and sinker (curls, blue eyes, and big smile).

For about one minute, she ate her popcorn and I chided myself for doubting her. I felt in control. I shopped for one minute before she started acting like Gretel, leaving a tiny popcorn trail. I calmly picked up piece after piece. I still felt like a capable mom.

Then we stopped to look at fancy socks for Easter. She has a sailor dress to wear. How sweet would white lacy socks be? No socks and more popcorn spilled. I picked it all up. By this time, my sweet girl was frantic because she dropped her fake lipstick in the back of the cart. She asked, "Back there?" to sit in the cart itself. I gave in and moved her to the back. Third mistake. This is when s#!t got real.

While talking to another mom, my little cutie dumped an entire bag of popcorn in the toy section. Why would I take her to the toy section?! And why hadn't I taken the popcorn by this time?? The other mom helped me pick up all the popcorn. And while this was happening, my girl tried to climb out of the cart. With one hand filled with popcorn, I wrapped my other arm around my daughter in a light wrestling hold. She hung on to my favorite necklace while pulling my shirt down. Another mom with very well-behaving kids came by and just smiled. Her kids looked like little blond cherubs.

Right around this time, my mischief-making girl spotted an Elsa microphone. "Let it go!" she yelled. To her delight, I grabbed it, marched to the checkout, and we left. I bought only the microphone. Survival.

And now I'm in the car, shaking. She's singing into her microphone. She won and I lost, and I realize I shouldn't have bought her a prize for her behavior. But I needed out of there and it seemed to be what I needed to do to make that happen.

Dear God. Let me raise this little redheaded wonder. Please. Amen.

If you've been that mom, I feel for you. Oh, I do. And to my favorite Target store, I promise I will never buy her popcorn again.

# TO THE POOR MOTHER

*L*

Two years ago I hit my rock bottom.

I remember feeling like there was no way we could slip any lower, but then we fell yet again. And when I was quite sure we were at rock bottom, in complete disbelief, one more time, we slipped a bit further until I was certain everything was about as bad as it could get.

My husband and I both had good jobs. But despite this, we still *just* made ends meet. Each month, by the grace of God, our growing family was able to thrive. But when you take one of those incomes completely away, I'm sure you can guess what happens.

I went through a postpartum depression after my third baby. I tried to go back to teaching simply because we needed my income, but I hurt so badly, crying constantly, just struggling to barely make it through my day. Not only the emotional but the physical pain I endured being away from my babies was so profound that I wouldn't wish it upon anyone.

Despite knowing what this was going to do to us financially, I knew I *needed* to be home with my babies.

So what was my turning point? How did I find my way forward?

We barely had any gas in my husband's vehicle. We still needed to plow through two more days before his payday. However, I'll never forget that night. I felt the deepest conviction that I needed to drive thirty minutes each way to take another mother, way more in need than we were, our double stroller. She had several young children, no vehicle, and many doctor appointments, and she was somehow walking all of her children to and from these appointments. The situation through which I learned of her was uncanny, but I was so blessed that I did.

I remember as I was sobbing in the shower one evening, literally soaking in self-pity and crying out to God for help and an answer to my problems, it quickly came to me.

I was overcome with the strongest urge to help this woman. I got out of the shower and told my husband I needed to take our stroller to her. Naturally, he questioned me, as we barely had enough gas for him to make it to work the next two days, let alone make an unexpected hour-long round-trip.

I couldn't explain to him my dire need to go help this mother, that it needed to be done right then. But I told him I needed to do this and out the door I went.

I don't remember many details from that night, including what the woman looked like or our exact exchange of words, but I do remember the feeling that this was exactly what I needed to do and that was my answer from God.

I asked for help for my family, and His answer to me was that we still were able to help. To *still* love. To *still* be selfless.

To *still* give. To *still* think of the needs of others. That there was still so much hurt, so much need, so much more than what we were going through.

After meeting this woman and handing over our double stroller, tears ran down my face in thanksgiving on the drive home. As I watched the fuel tank needle slip closer and closer to empty and knew that my husband would need to somehow make it to work the next day, right then and there I stopped worrying. I stopped trying to figure things out on my own. I was simply content with the fact that somehow, someway, things would just work out, as they always did.

It was then and there that I gave it all over to the One who had been patiently waiting for me to give it over to Him. To let Him fix things. To let Him do the impossible and turn our burdens into blessings. To pull us out of a hole that for so long had felt devoid of light.

If there is one thing I want to teach my children, it's about God's love and that we are merely instruments of His to be used. No matter what position we find ourselves in, there is always room to love, to help, to give.

So what is the secret to success? What is the key to finding true happiness? What is the answer to all the hurt, problems, and unfairnesses of this world?

It took endless years of struggle; countless periods of pain, depression, and solitude; and more occurrences of failure than I'd like to admit for me to finally accept the answer that was so plain and simple.

The key is to simply let go, let God, and give your will to

Him. And I promise you, each and every issue will receive its solution. Each and every desire will be answered, simply because your desires become His desires. Each and every question will be answered, but in His perfect timing and in His ideal way.

I'm grateful for every hardship we've endured as a family because those hardships, along with the poverty I experienced in my childhood, have taught me humility and given me an even deeper empathy for those less fortunate than myself.

Please remember: You're not a failure until you stop trying. I have learned that if I have no other testimony than "I'm still here," that is enough.

And, that, my friends, is what matters. By the grace of God, He's brought us out of our hole stronger, ready to serve Him more than ever. And each day I pray that He continues to increase my faith.

Big battles indicate big blessings are on their way.

Don't forget that no matter where we are in life, God has more in store. He never wants us to quit growing. He never wants to quit blessing us, simply because He wants us to pass on those blessings.

Today we catch ourselves selfishly complaining about a vehicle that our growing family barely fits in, but then we are quick to remember and thank God that we have our car to get us from point A to point B.

The nights someone complains about what is for dinner, we all praise Him that we have cabinets and a fridge filled with food to keep our babies' tummies full. And we pray that God sends an angel to all those families everywhere who are hungry and in need, just as He has sent numerous angels to help us. When we think we *need* this and that, I'm filled with gratitude that we were able to give items away for free to other families, and let me tell you how good that felt! Probably even better than being able to pay our bills on time.

As long as it took me to discover this secret of life, I'm so blessed that I did. I found out that another key to happiness—another key to success—is to always help bless others. THIS is why I consider myself rich sitting here today. And as a mother, there may be no greater truth I can teach my children.

Even when no one else notices or sees, He does. And He, in turn, blesses you. Even when the world says there is no way, God will find you a way.

Just be ready to take that path when He lays it out before you.

# DEAR MOM: THE SUN WILL SHINE AGAIN

*L*

We were dancing, lights flickering in the darkness, and her face was glowing in the shades of dark purples and blues. I took her hands in mine and said, "Are you happy? Like, really happy?" And she responded, "I am. I really am." Pulling me away from our dancing, she led me outside down a path covered in snow. The snow was so deep, but the sun was shining, and after the dark dance floor, I basked in the new light of day. At the end of the path, there was a beautiful strawberry patch. Huge, ripe strawberries were in abundance and she told me this was her patch; she had planted all of these berries and had been tending them despite the snow. She picked a huge berry for me and I took a bite, smiling at my luck to have such a wonderful friend who managed to grow strawberries despite the cold of winter.

And then I woke up.

That was my dream recently about a dear friend of mine. We've been friends for a long time and despite the fact that I hardly see her anymore because of the miles between my small Pennsylvania town and her location in the southwest, we are kindred spirits. Neither time nor distance can break a friendship like ours.

The dream was a needed reminder to me that there is nothing so constant as the changing of seasons and that despite the cold and dark of winter, spring and summer will come. Inevitably. Eventually. Winter will end. Always. And here it is summer. And sunny. And warm. Winter IS over.

Literally, this winter for us was brutal. My husband's schedule was erratic at best, and coupled with a rather challenging newborn, and the transitions occurring in our growing family, we felt like the winter would never end. Ever.

Metaphorically, I've just come out of my own dark winter. My life has been charmed, so my hardships are relative and I know it. But even as my head knew this, my heart truly focused on the day-to-day struggles, all minor. I wasn't the only one struggling; the friend mentioned above had her own struggles—much more complicated than my own. Actually, all around me people seemed to be suffering. There were a few friends whose grandparents or parents became ill and ultimately passed away. Others had sick kids, with one cold or flu after another. A coworker was fighting for her life. A friend was trying to get pregnant. Another was dealing with a toddler who was determined to make life with a new baby difficult. And yet another was trying to find a house to make a home in a new place. Everyone I knew seemed to be dealing with her own winter. And we all kept chugging along for the promise of the end and relief. We lifted one another up in friendship, and many of us prayed. And others meditated and tried to funnel good energy. And we made it. We did it. Prayer and these friendships sustained me.

Winter is over. Spring has passed. Summer is here. My dream, though, reminded me that there is a dance in the winter: The sweetest fruit can be found in that season, too!

# TO THE WIFE WHO LOST HER PASSION

*L*

The butterflies in your stomach, the romance, the nights that never end (and not because of children)—when you're in love, the world begins and ends with the two of you, and not anyone or anything can come between you.

Then comes parenthood, the biggest blessing and most incredible thing that can happen to a couple. However, too often, the couple that once was becomes subsumed in their new role as parents.

These six pieces of advice will help you keep the passion in your marriage afloat through parenting and beyond:

1. **Go Out of Your Way.** Why is it that so often we feel that the wooing stage—adoring and making your partner a priority—seems to slowly dissipate after the honeymoon is over? And then, when babies come into the picture, well, prepare to let your romance take a backseat to the needs of your family. Get comfortable, because it's going to be like this for a while. How do you get over this hump? Go out of your way to make time for your partner outside the demands of family. He will appreciate it, and it will remind you of the reason why you created your family in the first place.

2. **Be Available.** The kids are fed, bathed, and tucked into bed (more than likely, not their own bed). The mere fact that everyone just survived another day deserves a high five (maybe with a side of Pinot or Merlot). And then what? Where is the energy and passion and stamina left for your partner? The thought of dragging yourself into the shower sounds exhausting—never mind the thought of having the vitality for anything else. Be available in spite of this, and you'll surprise yourself with the passion it brings.

3. **Avoid Name-Calling During Disagreements.** Remember how they taught us as kids to "always fight nice"? Yeah, try telling yourself that when you're in the heat of the moment and ready to rip your spouse's head off—more than likely over something insignificant or a discussion that starts from indirectly talking to him through one of the kids in a passive-aggressive way: "*Oh my, isn't it funny that Daddy forgot to do this?*" Fast-forward five minutes, and you're gritting your teeth and mumbling that "*you know what*" name under your breath and giving your significant other the death look. Yeah, unfortunately, it happens.

4. **Say "I'm Sorry."** Why is it so hard to sometimes simply own up to our mistakes? Just fess up, man up, and claim responsibility. Acknowledge that yes, you made a mistake; yes, it's your fault; yes, you're sorry. Move on, together.

5. **Steer Clear of Family/Friend Drama.** Mind your

own business. If everyone in the entire world managed to do this simple thing, I think we would have a shot at world peace. Unfortunately, it's one of the hardest concepts for people to put into practice. If everyone would let a couple and their family decide what is best for *their* family and wait to be asked for their input (if, indeed, it's ever requested), there would be so much less drama. And let's face it: Who has time for drama?

6. **Never, EVER Drop the "D" Word.** No, it's not *diet*. The off-limit word is *divorce*. It's not something to toy with in arguments. No one goes to the altar planning or preparing for this. Why do we think it's okay to throw the idea around and threaten this so often and without thought? It's one word that should and needs to be taken out of every married couple's vocabulary—unless you really mean it.

Marriage ebbs and flows. Why? Because it's *alive*. As beautiful, fair, and lovely as it may sound, marriage will never be a 50/50 partnership. It might be close, but your partnership with your spouse will never come out to be exactly equal in terms of the amount of love being given, the amount of work being put in, or the amount of patience, compassion, forgiveness, understanding, and sensitivity shown toward the other at any given point in time. Despite that, seek comfort in this simple truth: While one person is possibly "checked out" or not capable of giving as much, be thankful that the other is able to hold on and love enough *for both of you*.

At the end of the day, I'm thankful that my marriage is never equal. When one of us is *done*, the other loves harder and salvages what many people might have found to be unsalvageable. We have overcome what the world says cannot be overcome.

Keeping the passion in your marriage alive after becoming parents isn't easy. To say it takes hard work is a massive understatement. That being said, the hard work and the sacrifices you make for the one you chose to spend forever with are well worth it. I praise God that despite the insanity of parenting, we are able to conquer and combat and be teammates in what is one of the most extraordinary yet difficult jobs in this world.

Family is forever. Just don't forget the person who started that family with you in the first place.

# DEAR MOM: KEEP YOUR HANDS OPEN

*L*

My son's school sits atop a hill and the view is breathtaking. On most days, I forget to notice. But this morning, the sun was making her way through the dark clouds. The sun's rays almost looked like fingers, spreading light through a sky colored in shades of red and orange. I said to my son, "Look. That is God's best work. That is God showing the world grace by allowing the sun to peak through the clouds. And the clouds are showing grace to the sun by allowing her to shine." I couldn't see his face, but I could sense his smile as he said, "That is so nice of God, Mama. That is so nice of the clouds."

My comment about grace to him was rooted in my own need for grace this morning. Last night, the baby didn't sleep well, again, and I was in and out of bed almost every two hours, like clockwork. I haven't been wearing exhaustion well, and in the haze of it, I yelled at my husband. Again. After we all fell back to sleep and I woke from a fitful rest, there was a text on my phone: "I'm sorry about last night. I love you." Not only did my husband extend grace, he also apologized for something out of his control. And I appreciated it. My soul needed his grace, and even though I hadn't apologized yet to him, he extended his hand.

Grace calls us to forgive, even if people aren't sorry or deserving. Grace calls us to turn the other cheek, as Jesus calls us to do. Extending grace is difficult and something that I haven't always been good at doing. At times, being right or feeling justified has been more important to me than showing grace.

Recently, I've felt ignored by an acquaintance. I have seen her numerous times around town, and she seemed literally to look away, refusing to acknowledge me. A few weeks ago, I sent her a message and asked if I had offended her. She didn't reply for over a week, then finally called and left a message. But by that time, I was angry. Hurt and placing blame, I didn't answer my phone and I didn't return her call. I could not extend grace or give her the opportunity to apologize. I could not and I would not. I kept my hands closed.

In the meantime, during that very same week, I was reminded of what it feels like not to be forgiven, to be judged, and to be the unwelcome recipient of loathing. It hurt, and despite my very best efforts to rectify the situation, grace was not extended to me. I reeled at how unfair the person was being and how he was holding on to anger.

Today, after my morning of reflection about grace and nature's example, I felt humbled. Who was I not to extend grace? God had forgiven me. My husband had forgiven me. I vowed to try harder to open my hands and extend grace.

God works in wonderful ways because, not even five minutes after the conversation with my son, I walked back out to the car, only to hear my name being called. I turned to see the mother whom I had reached out to a few weeks prior. She was rushing after me, explaining why she hadn't acknowledged me when she saw me. While she didn't quite say, "I'm sorry," I could tell she was, or at least she was sorry that I had hurt feelings. And I decided to extend grace. I looked at her and said, "Thank you," and "I understand."

It might seem small in the scheme of things, but I heard God's message today. It came from the grace my husband showed me, the grace God showed the world, and the grace the clouds showed the sun. I, in turn, passed it on and felt the healing power of extending it further.

# TO THE MOMMY WHO IS FIGHTING TO GET HER BODY BACK

*L*

My children are never going to remember how many push-ups I was able to do...

They won't remember how fast I was able to run a 5K...

They aren't going to remember what size I was...or wasn't, for that matter...

But they WILL remember that their mommy was strong.

That she was fierce.

That she believed in herself when nobody else did.

And despite all the times things got tough, insanely tough...

Despite all the times it would have been easier to quit, my children will remember that was when Mommy pushed harder.

I want my children to look back and say, "Because of my mommy, I never gave up."

IV.

# TO THE MOTHERS WHO WAIT

And we wait.

We wait for an answer.

We wait for a miracle.

We wait for the waters to be parted and for the mountains to move.

As we are trying to process the hundreds of emotions that come with finding out we are pregnant, why is it that all too often, and all too soon, so many of us are struck with such fear and anxiety over the most common burdens we face: the uneasiness of money and time. Sheer panic takes a tight hold on us, making us question how we are going to pay for this sweet baby on his or her way.

Not for lack of working hard, *no*. But because we are just making ends meet now. And then the slew of questions come from well-meaning loved ones: *Can you even afford another baby? How are you going to do this? You already work so much as it is; you're not even going to get time with your newborn, let alone raise him or her. How are you going to . . . well, do this?*

Yes, sadly all too often, as we are given the news of one of the greatest blessings that could be bestowed upon us, incessant questions from others follow that begin to take over our own thoughts, almost ripping the joy right out of our hearts.

As we continue through the pregnancy, our bellies grow as the unthinkable occurs—a human is growing inside us. A miracle is in the works—our baby is on her way. Our baby bump is surely growing, and then begin the sweetest kicks one could ever feel. Life is inside us, reminding us every single day that she exists.

As we begin to gather and prepare everything for this anticipated arrival, we also begin to prepare for what is the inevitable for millions of parents—the day we must leave our baby. The day we hand part of ourselves over to another. The day we will have to somehow muster up the inhuman strength to surrender a piece of our self, let go, and walk away.

At one point or another, we all will have to separate from our baby, no matter what age they are. That being said, some parents are forced to do this in an unfathomably short amount of time. When we look at the average leave being six to twelve weeks unpaid in the United States, for many, that would be a gift.

Mothers and fathers are resignedly handing over their "*x*"-day-old newborn—yes, *days* old—to another's care.

The first several weeks and months of an infant's life are a time of adjusting and the beginning of intense learning. Your baby is learning to open and close their big, bright eyes, lift their tiny hands, grasp with their fingertips, and lift their perfect, wobbly heads. They are learning the smells and the touch of the ones who are their caretakers, the ones who are essentially keeping this fragile and helpless baby alive.

They are learning how to suck, how to use their lungs, how to kick their legs up and down. They are learning what it feels like to be swaddled, what it feels like to be nuzzled, what it feels like to be soothed when they're upset, what it feels like to be caressed as they lay sleeping.

And parents are all too often robbed of these joys. Why?

For fear of losing our jobs.

For fear of not being able to put food on the table.

For fear of not being able to pay the rent.

For fear of having the hot water and the electricity shut off.

Yes, this fear is *very* real.

How would I know this? I've experienced it firsthand.

I know what it's like to have to dip into my babies' piggy banks to get groceries for the week. I know what it's like to be on your knees, praying to God that the utilities don't get turned off as the last few notices in the mail have stated they would. I know what it's like to lie awake at night as tears stream down your face, not knowing if you will be in your home the following month, and if you are, how the mortgage or rent is going to be paid.

I know what it's like to struggle, and worry, and lose out on what is supposed to be one of the most joyful times in our entire lives because despite being the most powerful country in the world, as a nation we overlook one of the most empowering times in a human being's life.

I know what it's like to work numerous jobs at once, trying

to show my children that they shouldn't expect anything to be handed to them, but yet so many times, I've come up short.

I know what it's like to hand over a newborn, not even being able to see clearly past the ocean of tears that have flooded my eyes. I know what it's like to walk out the door and have a pain that I will never fully be able to explain—to anyone. God is the only one who will ever know the true ache that I and millions of others have experienced, both physically *and* emotionally.

And so, we wait.

We *still* wait for an answer.

We *still* wait for a miracle.

We are *still* waiting for the waters to be parted and for the mountains to move.

I don't write this begrudgingly since it's too late for me, four babies later. But I write this with hope. I write this with a big faith. I write this knowing that we will have congressmen step up and do what is right. I write this knowing that God will both open and change the hearts of mayors and CEOs to take this issue upon themselves. I write this with the certainty that we will continue to have a United States secretary of labor who will fight and plead for us, for this cause, for this right—to have paid maternity leave.

Almost 4 million babies are born each year in the United States.

Approximately 334,000 babies each month.

Approximately 11,000 babies every single day.

Each day, thousands of parents and babies are experiencing the epitome of joy, the sheer essence of experiencing and basking in a true miracle. And yet every single day, thousands of parents are finding themselves one day closer to the heartache of leaving their infant in someone else's care, a valiant and painful undertaking.

If you want something to change, you have to *do* something different. Without change, progress is impossible.

Year after year, baby after baby, I went through distraught days that turned into weeks that turned into months and yes, years—such physical and emotional pain as a result of being forced back to work because of not having a paid leave. I cried out to God for an answer and selfishly questioned and prayed at times, *"Why can't it be different for me?"*

I now know why. I needed to be a strong voice for millions. To cause waves. To be a fighter for what our country's parents deserve. To believe and campaign for those parents who are unable to find any hope that this can change for them.

You can do what I cannot do. I can do what you cannot do. And together we can do great, incredible things.

And so we wait.

But we will not wait quietly.

We will not wait submissively.

We will no longer wait fearfully.

We will fight together until we are heard.

# DEAR MOM: YOUR ARMS ARE THEIR HOME

*L*

My daughter said, "I'm home with Mommy," and snuggled her head into my shoulder on this late August day. She had started school two days before. She had a great two days, but when this day was over, all she wanted was to be held in my arms.

Together with my son, we were at the park they both love, right in the middle of the chaos of many children running and laughing. My daughter, usually one to love the park (and beg to go!), mostly wanted me to carry her around instead of playing with her brother. Today, my arms were her safe place. And I marveled at how, for my sweet girl, my arms are her home.

No matter where we are, she takes refuge in them. No matter what time of day, she knows I'll hold her. I'm her safe haven, her constant, her home. And I delight in holding her whenever she needs me to.

Even as my son is getting older, there are days he still asks me to hold him. And when we got home from the park, he did. I think he saw how much I was holding his sister. So I was quick to oblige. His legs are getting so long, and I can't pick him up and carry him because my arms quickly tire under his newfound weight. These days of carrying him are over, much like these last days of summer that will soon turn into the crispness of fall, the leaves falling from the trees in shades of amber and rust. So, while I can't carry him around like I do his sister, he does crawl into my lap. When he finds his spot, like he has for many years, he draws his arms around my neck and we sit like that for a while. And today, his sister ran over to join us.

Like always, I asked him why he wanted me to hold him so much. He leaned back, his fading blond temples made blonder by the light coming in from the back window, his gray eyes serious. He said, "It's because your arms feel like home." My heart melted at the poetry in his words, ones I have heard him say before. My arms are home for these children of mine. There is no better compliment, no greater gift, no greater job, no more important purpose. As I cuddled him and his sister on my lap, I whispered to them both, "Your arms feel like my home, too."

We moms, with our imperfections and insecurities, have the great privilege of being home for our children, our arms their very sanctuary.

# DEAR POSTPARTUM DEPRESSION

*L*

It's no secret or surprise; babies bring such anticipation, joy, and an unexplainable love upon their arrival. They bring a whole new meaning to your life's happiness and touch places deep in your heart that you never even knew existed.

But it's not always smiles, happy tears, or a walk in the park. How I wish it were, but that just isn't the case. When we begin this journey of becoming pregnant, right then and there we are turning our bodies over. Right then and there we are living, eating, breathing, and existing for someone else. Every decision we make, everything we do, everywhere we go, we are not alone, and it's a safe assumption to make that from this time forward, there will never be a day that goes by that we won't worry or second-guess ourselves.

After the baby arrives you will feel such amazement, grandeur, and pride that this little perfect person came from you and now belongs to you. But with that comes a constant apprehension concerning how and what you're doing. You question each and every move you make and endure endless worry that something is or could go wrong.

And then for some, without warning, you might slip into an unfamiliar, dark, life-altering place.

I'll never forget the words echoing throughout the doctor's office. It was almost as if I was ready to turn around to look for a woman being diagnosed behind me. I had researched it, I knew it, I certainly felt it, but to actually hear the words out loud, being said to me, was crushing. I felt defeated. I felt so small. I felt helpless. I almost felt as if I were ruined. But most of all, I just felt lost. Postpartum depression. Me? Impossible.

This was my third baby. Sure, I had anxiety and hormones that were all over the place after I delivered my first and second babies, but this—this was something different. Although it was all mental and emotional, it very well may have been one of the worst physical pains my body had ever endured.

One of the biggest challenges I encountered was the lack of a response to my question "So when is 'this' going to be gone? I'm done with it already and just want this nightmare to be over with, for good." Unfortunately, there was no magic wand that could be waved over me or a magic pill, for that matter, to make this hurt disappear. Everyone kept telling me I was "fine." "You're okay...just try to snap out of it. Just be happy. You are going to be fine." If one more person tried to dismiss or underplay not only my pain but, more so, the devastation I felt, I thought I would snap. I wasn't fine. I wasn't okay, and I feared that the next person who told me how I was supposed to feel would end up with a punch to the nose.

The thing that crushed me most with this diagnosis was the stigma attached to postpartum depression. Half of me was just plain humiliated for anyone to know what I was facing every single moment of every single day, and the other half of me felt such anger and resentment and self-pity, I was ready to go up and share my sob story with the woman behind me in line to check out at the grocery store.

Was this just me? What did I do? How could I have been so weak that I let myself slip into this almost coma-like state that I was terrified I'd never wake up from?

I remember the first time an acquaintance questioned my diagnosis: "Well, isn't that where you want to hurt your baby? I mean, could you really ever want to hurt your baby?" To be completely honest, I can't quite remember just how I responded. I do know that I paused for quite some time and had to lift my jaw up from the floor. I was in such disbelief that someone could have the audacity to say such a thing, because for me, it was the furthest thing from truth. But as unfortunate as it is, our society is terribly misinformed about the gaping difference between postpartum depression and postpartum psychosis. And because of this, many women silently suffer for fear of humiliation and of being judged as "crazy," or, even worse, as a bad mother.

I never had one single thought or urge to shake or hurt my baby in any way, shape, or form. In fact, I was the exact opposite. I suffered severe anxiety when I was away from my children; I agonized over the thought of being separated from them. One thinks of childbirth as being painful, but comparatively, this, the emotional and physical trauma I felt encompassing my entire body, was by far the deepest pain I had ever endured.

My days varied. Sometimes I tried to put on the happiest face I could muster. Other days, anyone who saw me could see the turmoil I was experiencing. One of the most unnerving "places" of this entire experience was when I felt a mood but I couldn't decipher if I was putting on a front or if that was actually how I felt. I found myself internalizing: *I am smiling right now, but is it even sincere? Am I actually somewhat complacent?* Or there were times I wondered if I really wanted to get better. There were points when I was so down that there seemed to be no "getting better" in sight. It was so easy to lose my grasp on all the positives in my life. Every single negative, no matter how tiny, seemed more significant than any good thing within my reach.

Almost twenty months later, after giving birth to my third child, I naturally still face tough days, just as every other human being does. I hurt, I cry, I vent, I get angry, and at times, I bathe in hideous self-pity, asking, "Why me? How can I keep going with everything on my plate?"

For so long I questioned and prayed and begged for this hurting to be over, but for what seemed an endless period of time, it was still there the next day. I can't tell you the exact turning point or the defining moment that swept me off the desolate island I felt I was living on, but I do remember starting to see, feel, and experience more good days than bad.

As any woman who has gone through this can relate, to feel normal and whole once again takes time. But there was a moment *I came to.* One evening, I realized I hadn't thought about feeling bad that whole day. I was overcome, in tears, grateful. *I have bravely beaten this hideous beast*, I thought. It was amazing to simply recognize ME again.

It felt good to smile and not have to force it. It felt good to laugh because I wanted to laugh. It felt good to notice and seek out so many of the incredible, positive things in my life. But it felt even more amazing to see my babies look at me as if they saw a new person. A familiar, yet happier person they hadn't seen in such a long time. I felt whole again.

You will too.

## TO THE MOM GIVING THANKS

*L*

On our walk last night, we stopped in at our friends' home. We live in the sort of small town where people still visit after dinner on front porches, sidewalks, and in backyards. It's what I love about living here—the casual, impromptu meetings, the gathering of friends to make sense of our days. After chatting on the front porch for a few minutes, watching the two older kids whiz by us on their scooters, flashes of blond hair catching my attention with each race, my friend took me into her backyard to give me some of her mint. After cutting some for me, I traded the armload of my almost one-year-old daughter for the handful of mint. I smelled it—caught up in its wonderful scent and promise of mint sweet tea, one of my favorites. I was happy, too, to be free of my little girl for a moment and her new habit of biting my arm and shoulder when I hold her. My friend, now the mother of a seven-year-old daughter, breathed in her newfound handful, too. Their hair, almost the same strawberry blond color, caught the fading sun's rays, and they both looked at peace. She held my daughter close, eyes closed, and said, "She smells like the ocean." The beauty of her words and observation hung in the air. I smiled at her, lost in my own thoughts.

My daughter will be one soon. I prayed for her conception; I begged for her; I cried about her. After years of dreaming of having a baby girl, I finally received her. I've always known her, even before she was formed. I would see women with their daughters in their arms and wonder when I would be given my daughter. I knew that she would take her daddy's heart, twisting it until it hurt, and get her way every time. I knew that she would be tenacious, outgoing, and adventurous. I could see her in dreams as she toddled through our house, creating havoc with every step. I knew her, but I wasn't given her right away. And, over time, I became content with that. Instead, I was blessed with a son. My son was all I had ever hoped or dreamed for in a child. The dream of a daughter was pushed to the back of my mind. But then my son started to pray for a baby sister each night. The first night he did, I was taken aback. I hadn't ever spoken to him about my dream for a little girl. But he knew. His soul knew her, too, and it was as if he had known her before and was just waiting for her arrival. He was so sure. And so my prayer turned, and I asked God to not only send me a daughter but also to send my son his sister.

I believe in answered prayers. I see one in my sweet girl, who sat content last night in the arms of my friend and who is now peacefully asleep as this summer storm blows through. I sit now and say a silent prayer of gratitude for this daughter of mine—this one who smells like the ocean asleep in her crib. I now pray that our love for her surrounds her, as the ocean does an island, its waves lapping on the shore, helping the shoreline take shape. I pray that our arms become her respite, the safe harbor for a little girl from the ocean's tumultuous waves. I pray that she one day explores the wide world, confident, because really, the ocean will find its match in the brave woman she will become. My prayer is that this sister knows how her brother adores her. I hope this baby girl knows how her daddy's heart swells when she calls his name. I pray that this daughter of mine, with her big blue eyes, knows that my love for her is limitless, too.

# TO THE MOM WHO FORGETS WHAT CHILDHOOD IS ABOUT

*L*

I feel confident enough to say I'm living proof that it isn't the quantity but the quality of time I get with my children that counts.

But...is that it? Work, work, work. Pay the bills, keep everyone alive and thriving? As long as the money is coming in, that should be more than enough, right?

Wrong.

Is our children's happiness, *true* happiness, found within how much money is spent on them? Is your daughter going to remember that outrageously priced dress you bought for her that she wore for a little over an hour? Is your son going to think you're the best parent ever for putting on an over-the-top themed birthday bash every single year (where you put more time into impressing the people coming than into actually creating some special moments with your child on his special day)? Will you be considered parent of the year for continually taking your children on lavish trips that more times than not stress everyone out, leaving them sleep-deprived and frustrated to the point that despite all you have saved and now spent, everyone is more than ready to go home?

Will our children be happy only if we throw every toy, every electronic device, every want and desire they have right at their feet? Do our kids get their security and pleasure from our giving them things versus giving them of ourselves?

What does it cost to take your kids on a nature walk? To chase them around the yard? What does it cost to play tag and hide-and-seek? What does it cost to play catch, push your child on a swing, or give a piggyback ride? What does it cost to ride a bike, play a board game, color a picture, or read an extra book? What does it cost to put down your phone or iPad and give your child your undivided attention when they have something to tell you? What does it cost to have imaginary play, take a trip to the park, share an ice cream cone, or *be* a kid *with* your kid?

Take their shoes off. Let them run around in their bare feet and feel the earth beneath them. Load them up with sunscreen and play out in the fresh air as long as their little hearts desire. Let them get dirty, jump in puddles, and dance in the rain. And better yet, surprise them and really give them something to remember when you double their joy by joining them.

You can see that all these things have one thing in common. They cost nothing yet are worth *everything*. These are the things your children will remember and cherish most. You can't put a price tag on any of them, though their worth can easily be labeled as priceless.

I always go back to my checklist of asking if my children are safe, happy, healthy, and *know* how much they are loved even if every day I lose my patience and raise my voice. If I am able to check off all the positives, then I can go to sleep feeling content.

Remember, it's the little things. The *simple* things. But mainly, it's *you*. All they want is you. If you can give your children that, you're giving them everything.

I was going to vacuum and fold laundry. If I had, I would've missed my life as it happened—my kids running through the sprinkler in the fading sun on a warm spring evening.

It was a sunny, warm day, not typical weather for April where we live. The sun flooded through the windows, illuminating every single crumb that might have gone unnoticed on a cloudy day and the crumbs were really all I could focus on, along with the laundry on the sofa. All I could think was, *How are there so many crumbs here? How am I the only one to notice them? Where did all of that laundry come from?*

It was clear the house needed to be vacuumed. Among other things, there were crumbled tortilla chips on the kitchen floor, left where my daughter threw then stepped on them when I was loading the dishwasher after dinner. I saw them a few times, basking in the sunlight, taunting me. And I kept thinking, *After dinner, I will vacuum.* The laundry needed to be folded and put away, and I kept thinking, *After dinner, I will fold the laundry.*

But after dinner, my husband gave the kids each a popsicle and excitedly asked them if they wanted to go run through the sprinkler. His question was immediately met with cheers from both kids. My son cheered because he knows how fun running through a sprinkler is on a hot day; my daughter, always one for a celebration, cheered and clapped because her brother already was doing both. She even started singing and moving her shoulders up and down to the beat of the song she was singing.

The kids ran off with my husband to get their bathing suits while I got the vacuum from the closet and brought it into the kitchen, walking past the pile of laundry in the other room.

I could hear them laughing upstairs as they hurriedly put on their bathing suits. I smiled and laughed, too. *Why am I missing out on the fun?* I wondered. They came down and headed outside. I decided the vacuuming and the laundry could wait, and I followed them outside and sat in the grass.

My husband and I sat in the sun with a cup of coffee and laughed and clapped along with our children. My daughter's joy was contagious. She ran through the sprinkler with no fear, and when she got to the other side, she clapped and jumped up and down, the biggest smile on her face. I looked at my husband and smiled at him, too.

In a sea of obligations, worries, meltdowns, crumbs, and laundry, we had a perfect five minutes. Life doesn't always look like this for us, but I'm noticing when it does and saying my thanks for it.

There once was a time when I had a spotless house, but I wonder how many everyday moments I missed while I fought to maintain that perfection. I once didn't have piles of laundry anywhere and you could always count on my house to be in near perfect condition.

Listen, Mama, I know we can't witness every single moment. It's impossible for any of us. Sometimes, we need to work or rest or clean. But that warm April evening, I almost missed out on the joy I didn't need to miss out on at all. Sometimes, our homes can stay messy. Sometimes, the crumbs can stay on the floor. Sometimes, the laundry simply must wait.

Friend, if you can, put aside something that can wait in order to see the beauty right in front of you. Give yourself permission simply to enjoy your life.

$\mathcal{L}$

When my son was six, he was completely obsessed with *Star Wars*, much like my own brother was when I was a little girl. He was Darth Vader for Halloween and his baby sister, only an infant at the time, was Princess Leia. When we re-did his baby bedroom at age four, he was insistent on a *Star Wars* theme. And even though he was young, I'd allow him to watch parts of the movies from time to time, because I do believe the movies tackle tough topics and give us opportunities to discuss them, having the hard talks together and not leaving them up to someone else to have when I'm not around. When he was young, I know we covered a few things some parents might be uncomfortable talking about, but in the end, it's just helped my son learn more about empathy.

One rainy day, when his baby sister was napping and I had laundry to fold, I allowed him to watch a *Star Wars* movie because he had been so sweet to his sister, who was sick with a cold. As I folded laundry, I said something to him like, "Geez, I think Darth Vader is really creepy." I expected my comment to be met with, "Yeah, Mama, he really is." But instead, my son looked at me with incredulous eyes, his mouth hanging wide open, as if I had insulted a friend. He said, "Mama, I think Darth Vader has some good in him. I know he's on the bad side, but I don't think he's all bad." And this movie spurred a discussion about good versus evil, the church, and how goodness is in everyone if we only look closely enough.

All around me, I feel like I've been faced with examples of people not being on their best behavior. Day after day, I encounter people who seem rude for no obvious reason. Someone ran into my cart in the grocery store and didn't apologize; a person with the gas company was rude to me on the phone when I called about a question on our bill. My son seems always to be watching and listening, and so when I got off of the phone with the gas company, I said to my husband, "Wow. She was so rude." My sweet boy said, "Mama, remember what you always tell me. We all have bad days and can only be nice to people when they're having one."

Through our days together, my children teach me so many lessons. And that day—the day we watched the *Star Wars* movie—he reminded me that all we can do is to treat people the way we want to be treated.

His words served as reminder to me that I, too, have said things I've regretted later. Maybe the woman at the gas company was exhausted from so many calls and needed a break and a hot cup of tea. The woman who ran into us in the grocery store and didn't apologize could have been lost or maybe she received some bad news. I won't ever know. I do know those people weren't showing their best sides, but I know I've been in their shoes. We all have. We all say things we regret. We all act too quickly and do something we wish we hadn't. And, if we are lucky, we are met with the kindness of a person who knows what it's like simply to have a bad day.

My son has always reminded me that good is in everyone and he's taught me to try harder to see it. Now, I try hard to smile when met with a frown. I try hard to extend the hand when people aren't being the nicest. Because, like he said, even Darth Vader has good in him.

# TO THE MOM FALLING APART

*L*

Quickest way to tear down an entire family? Take out the mother.

After having my fourth baby in six years, I was preaching the need to take care of oneself. Of course, after learning the hard way. I believed in this fully because it's just a proven fact that when the mother goes down, the entire household goes down with her.

I didn't realize how foolish I had been, driving myself into the ground, until I was driving myself to the hospital after being sick for six straight weeks. There I was, deathly ill, barely able to hold my head up, and yet I was actually somewhat enjoying myself. No kids in the car, the music turned up, feeling as if I had gotten a small break.

Back up. Something is *very* wrong with that picture.

When the hospital staff asked me why I waited this long, letting myself get so ill, naturally my response was, "Well, I have four young children. There's really no right time to come. I just...didn't have the time."

I watched their eyes go back and forth to each other, half in pity and half thinking how absurd it sounded, and I thought to myself, *I have four young children. What the hell was I thinking? All the more reason to make sure I take care of myself!*

When I got back home, I became even more grateful to have a warrior of a partner to help combat the chaos and craziness of a busy house that does not stop or slow down when Mommy can no longer *go*. For a hardworking husband who already more than carries his weight, taking on the duties of almost the entire household brings with it the *"Oh, CRAP"* moments. I watched my poor husband and listened from the monitor as he tried to tackle the needs of a six-year-old, a four-year-old, a two-year-old, and a five-month-old while I was stuck in bed, unable to lift my head.

I've changed diapers with one eye open and nursed a baby that I could barely hold because my strength was so lacking. I've had an emotional breakdown in front of the doctor, my son's preschool teacher, and the UPS man. Yeah, the poor delivery guy just trying to get on with his day. Who does that, right?

An overly emotional, extremely sick, completely exhausted, and physically drained mother. And who or what did I owe this to?

Myself.

Throughout these trying times, I've discovered that marriage and parenting are never 50/50. And you know what? Thank God for that. There are so many times when one of us feels as if we're giving more than "our share," but the truth of the matter is, when one of us isn't able to give our usual portion, the other makes up for it. And that's the pure beauty and absolute phenomenon of the ever-changing and ever-unequal balance in this thing called **family**.

Come on, it's not easy dealing with the chick who hasn't showered in two … three (okay, I'll leave it at three) days. You get the hug at the door, "Mmmm, same outfit as yesterday, honey? Excellent!" The already hormonal roller-coaster ride takes even deeper dips through the sickness and exhaustion, and all one can do is buckle up and hold on for dear life.

Let's face it. Who has time to be sick? What mother has time to be sick? What mother of four tiny children has any minutes penciled in for THIS to go down?

NO ONE has time to be sick, especially not a mother of four.

There are times I feel like I could stand on top of the roof and throw my hands high in the air as my superhero cape blows in the breeze and scream a fierce "YESSSS!" On so many occasions we are able to accomplish and conquer, well, the unthinkable.

But there are other times, in order to be able to do what others say is impossible, we must give our body the break that it is crying out for.

I realized that sometimes life doesn't allow us to keep the superhero cape on. And as hard as it is to swallow that pill, sometimes turning over the job and letting someone else step in is what makes for a real superhero.

Admitting that we can't. Admitting that we have nothing left. That our tank is more than empty, and we can't give one single ounce more.

Maybe *that* is a superhero mother?

To open your mouth and utter the words "I can't. I just can't. I need...help." It's like a cut into the mother ego of the unrealistic thoughts we possess that we need to and should be doing it all.

And frankly, no one else will do it as good as Mommy does. Right?

I'm someone who likes to be in control. I like to be able to fix everything and pick up all of the pieces. No one bathes the kids like Mommy; no one brushes their teeth and dresses them like Mommy does. No one rubs heads to sleep like I do; nor does anyone else know how the kids like their milk poured, their sandwiches cut in that special way, and their favorite, most comfortable way to be held and picked up.

But the truth is, when we run ourselves into the ground, when we know that our family is actually suffering because of our inability to accept or seek help, it's a problem for everyone.

I did this to myself. I did this to my family, simply forgetting to take care of number one. And it took many hits, many collapses, many times of hitting rock bottom before I learned that it's okay if I can't give 24 hours a day, 7 days a week, 365 days a year.

As mothers we are built to endure like no other. We are equipped with supernatural forces that allow us to push on when it seems impossible to push on. We are composed of every healing word, touch, and remedy.

But bottom line, we're still human. And sometimes we forget that.

We do make mistakes. We do tire. We can get pulled down. We do become annoyed (yes, dear heavenly Father, You know this). We live and breathe for our children and would walk across fire for them, but yes, we do require a break from them at times. And you know what? They need a break from us, too. They need the opportunity to become more independent and well-rounded human beings and learn how to function and cope and perform and accomplish *without* Mommy right there.

Swallowing our pride and admitting to that may very well be the hardest thing we superhero mothers have to do.

The harsh reality is, we won't be there to prevent our child's every fall. We won't be able to shield them from every heartache, or fight every battle for them. Sometimes we need to take a step back and let them learn some independence, test out their wings on their own, so one day they will be ready to fly when it's time. And *when* that time does come, whether we're ready for it or not, we don't want them to be hesitant but rather to confidently go after their dreams and goals and bravely face their challenges.

Through this period of exhaustion and illness that befell me, I was able to find the silver lining. That's the beautiful thing about these so-called setbacks. In each and every storm, there is a lesson to be learned. And when the sunshine does return, you know the rainbow is not far off.

So when Mommy was down for the count, did my family have their struggles? Sure. Did things move a little less smoothly? Yes. Were my husband and children excited for me to bounce back? Absolutely.

But let me tell you: During that time, my family learned to overcome and rally together as a team. Our toddlers even learned more independence, and a bonus sense of nurturing and caring for one another as well.

Sadly, I have had this happen after each baby at some point, so I must never have fully learned my lesson. I have hit rock bottom multiple times through the past seven years of motherhood. But here I am, four babies later, still learning. Still needing my daily wake-up calls. Still being reminded that it takes a village. Still requiring the blunt slap in the face that tells me, *Nope, you can't do it all, and you know what . . . that is okay.*

So next time you're pushing way too hard, flying past the big red flashing sign that reads "WARNING, DANGEROUS TERRITORY AHEAD," put on the brakes and ask yourself, *Who am I doing this for?*

When the leader is down, the family learns new and different ways of combat. They learn to operate at an entirely new level of strong that they never knew existed. They learn what true teamwork and responsibility are. They learn that when a person must step up, he or she is capable of more than anyone ever thought. That's what my family learned. And yours can, too.

I've decided that I don't need to be Superwoman any longer. I don't need anyone else's approval or rating of the job I'm doing at home. I no longer desire to please everyone. I've found that the several thousand times I've attempted this, I've consistently pedaled backward.

No, I no longer want to be Superwoman. I just need five sets of eyes within my household to know I'm there. That I'm taking care of myself so in turn, I can take care of them. I need these five beating hearts to realize I love them with an insurmountable love they'll never come close to knowing the depth of. I need to be strong for these five people; I want them to think that I am their Superhero, whether or not I'm doing it all. If I have their approval, I must be doing something right.

So...what's the quickest way to tear down an entire family?

Yep, take down the mother.

But it's also the quickest way to rally your family, your team, and watch them grow!

# TO THE MAMAS WHO ALLOW THEM TO "DO IT"

*L*

"I do it!" These are the words I hear, over and over again, all day long.

When we're rushing out the door, I hear these words when you try to buckle your own shoes. I stop to help you and you say, "I do it!" And I let you do it, even though it's frustrating, because I know someday your little shoes won't be at the door at all. So I wait and watch you slowly buckle them, and I try to savor the moment of watching your tiny feet fit into those shoes.

Every morning before the sun is up or before I've made my own coffee, I grab a glass from the cabinet and the orange juice from the fridge, but even before I take the cap from the container, you say, "I do it!" So I sit you on your stool and watch with tired eyes as you so carefully pour the juice into the cup. And at first, you spilled the juice and I tried very hard not to sigh. But now, you can pour almost perfectly, and the small smile you give me tells the story of your pride.

And yesterday, when I took off your life vest after you waded in the bay, you yelled, "I do it!" when I started to fasten the vest back up to put it away. So we sat and you slowly fastened the vest without pinching your fingers—that was my worry and I tried to explain that to you, but you just kept saying, "I do it." And you did it. And you didn't pinch your fingers at all. I watched you fasten this literal life vest, and my mind couldn't help but to go to a figurative life vest. Right now, my arms are that for you, daily, but before long, they won't be. So yesterday, I just watched you buckle it—your chubby hands working—and nothing seemed so important. And where was I rushing to, after all?

Shoes and orange juice and life vests are all obstacles in your path, and every time you are able to persevere over one, your confidence grows. And I need to help you learn that you really can do it. To a two-year-old, the world can be a frustrating place; I forget that sometimes. And so, today, I want to honor your need to say, "I do it!" By doing so, I'm showing you that you can do anything you set your mind to as long as you have the patience to try.

# A NOTE TO THE MOTHER
# QUESTIONING MOTHERHOOD

*L*

I've traded my house that was once quiet and in order for complete chaos and disorganization.

I've traded my nights of sleep for days of exhaustion.

I've traded my once voluptuous chest for, well, business...almost a decade of working boobs.

I've traded late nights out at the bar for late nights pacing the hall.

I've traded my lightweight and trendy purse for a diaper bag so big it barely fits in my vehicle.

I've traded a tight, muscular body for one where everything has moved, shifted, and appeared in places it never was before.

I've traded being on time for giving fashionably late a whole new meaning.

I've traded a normal workout some days for simply loading and unloading, buckling and unbuckling, and going in and out of the house with four kids. It gives Shaun T a run for his money. This is my definition of INSANITY.

I've traded falling asleep to my favorite Bravo reality shows for passing out during *Dora, Mickey Mouse, Sophia,* and *Peppa Pig*...the episode I've watched for the twelfth time.

I've traded my stylish and tasteful wardrobe for wearing the same outfit for days in a row, my finest from the clearance rack.

I've traded the bed I once shared with just my husband for one sometimes filled with the entire family.

I've traded my heels for some flats... Who am I kidding? I'm barefoot most days.

I've traded long, luxurious showers for a two-minute rinse-off with little people either trying to bust down the door or sticking their fingers underneath it to try to reach me.

I've traded my sanity for... well, a whole lotta crazy.

I've traded long hair that was always straightened, curled, or styled for a greasy bun thrown on top of my head.

I've traded a clean, crumb-free kitchen for a feeding barn that never seems to close or appear to be sanitary.

I've traded a flat stomach for a soft spot that my babies like to rest their heads upon.

I've traded frequent date nights out with my husband for watching a show played back on the DVR before one of us is summoned.

So basically, I've traded easy for hard, well-rested for draining, and carefree for anxious.

So *this*... *this* is motherhood?

As crazy as it may be to believe, I think I'll take it.

To be honest, this zoo, this complete chaotic circus with its never-ending responsibilities, was, quite frankly, the easiest trade-off of my life.

$\mathcal{L}$

I try hard to write notes to my children every day before school and place them in their lunch boxes. It's not always easy to remember, but I have a system down and try to write short and simple notes, tucked away in their lunch boxes for only them to see at lunchtime. My daughter's notes are mostly just small hearts on Post-it notes because she can't read. And, on my son's I mostly write, "I love you." I write them because I want the kids to have a small piece of me and of home with them while at school. Honestly, the process is as much for me as it is for them.

When I first started this practice with my son in kindergarten, I didn't think he cared too much about my notes because for the first two months, he didn't say anything about them other than to thank me for writing them. But one day after school, I noticed the small pocket on the front of his newly purchased and monogrammed lunch box was unzipped. Upon closer inspection, I found all of the notes I'd ever written him. They were all there—the funny ones and the simple ones with hearts. He had saved every single one. When I asked him why he had saved them, he told me that sometimes, when he's at lunch, he'll read through all of my notes. As a teacher myself, I can't volunteer at his school for lunch duty. He told me that sometimes seeing the other moms there made him homesick.

I hugged him tight. He smiled at me and said, "It's okay, Mama. The notes always remind me how you love me and how you're in my heart."

In the spaces between our morning departure—the note writing, the making of lunches, the ironing of shirts, the last hugs before the kids begin their days—and the end-of-the-day "Hey, Mom" and our family roundtable discussion about the favorite parts of the day, to bedtime snuggles, these children are never far from me. They're right in my heart and I am in theirs. And the notes help us remember.

Sometimes, as mothers, we wonder if the small things really matter to the people we love. They do, Mama. So keep on putting those letters in their lunchboxes whenever you remember.

# TO THE MOM PRACTICING PEACE

*L*

The horrors of the world have been weighing heavily on my mind. So today, I tried to practice peace in my own home. It might not have solved anything, but I did my best to surround my small family with love while the world seems to be seething. Peace is such a powerful vehicle for change. Practicing peace, in my own small way, seemed like the thing to do today. *No more war.*

No more war. This resonates with me in all areas of life. No more war with my husband. No more war with myself. No more war with my body image. No more war with my critics. No more war. Today, I wave the peace flag and gracefully bow out. This is so hard to do, but I'm simply tired of a lifetime of waging war—the war to be justified, to stay thin, to keep a perfect house, or to be the perfect parent. The war to be understood. Most of my battles are internal, and war is making me its forever enemy.

Recently, my husband and I were having a mild disagreement. Our son brought a ball to us and said, "This is the peace ball. You each need to take it and when the other has it, you listen. This is how you practice peace." While we were still more than a little annoyed with one another, we did our best in that moment for our sweet boy. My husband threw in some sarcasm, which made us laugh, and in that way, the peace ball helped to lighten the burden of our fight. Even if it didn't take away the issues, we were pleasant enough in the moment. For the moment, no more war.

Later, my son told my aunt about this, and, together, they made peace rocks. They picked out some rocks, wrote "Peace" in color on them, and he passed them out. What a sweet and wonderful thing to do—a small gesture showing that he chose peace. What if, instead of waging war in its many forms, we chose peace? What if we passed the peace rose like they do in my son's school, or we just said, "No more war"? So many conflicts could be avoided by those three actions. I'm going to do my best to wave the peace flag. I might fail on some days and in some ways; but today, I choose no more war. And I'm lucky that I can.

War is being waged everywhere, every day—inside ourselves and in our homes, outside our doors and in our schools, grocery stores, and churches. It's the war of insecurity and hurt. It's the war of hate and bigotry. It's the war of superiority and misunderstanding. I wish it were simple enough to pass the peace rose, peace ball, or peace rock, among ourselves and to others, but I realize it isn't always that simple. What could we solve if we left war, in its many forms, off our tables, out of our hearts and homes? No more war. No more war. No more war.

Let us all pray for peace today. Peace in our own hearts. Peace and the calm after the storm.

V.

# TO THE MOM TEACHING HER CHILD TO TRY HARDER

*L*

"If you don't want to swim, don't swim," said the beautiful older woman with sparkling blue eyes and long gray hair. I remember her hair because she was fixated on mine, stroking my long brown hair as she spoke to me, her blue eyes piercing my green ones. We weren't anywhere near a swimming pool, and I had no idea at the time what she really meant by the words. She was an Alzheimer's patient, and I heard her words well before I ever became a mother. We were visiting my husband's grandfather in a hospital wing for Alzheimer's patients, and the woman was drawn to me; the nurse thought I must have reminded her of someone. And so I sat, letting her stroke my hair, as she kept repeating her words about swimming, and stopping to grab my face to stare into my eyes. Since then, I have thought of her words as a metaphor—don't do things you don't want to do—but lately, I've been applying them in my life with my son.

My son is almost six, and he cannot swim. I've literally echoed her words: "If you don't want to swim, don't swim." But it's a matter of safety, so he must learn how to swim. If he doesn't want to swim, fine, but he **must** know how. Despite our best efforts to teach him to swim, he is simply terrified of the water. Once, when he was two, we went to the beach and our accommodations had an inground pool with a fence around it. My son wouldn't even step foot inside the fence. We cajoled, bribed, and finally got him to stand inside the fence on the very last day. He screamed the entire time—the entire two minutes—until we were afraid we were traumatizing him. So we thought, *We'll try again later*.

Later came when we enrolled him in a swim class the following year. My husband got in the pool with him for the "mommy and me" swim classes. My son was three and the other children were mostly babies. He still just held tightly to my husband. He wouldn't even try to swim.

And we really didn't push it. We just kept him in floating devices, and he's never been in the water without an adult. This has gone on year after year, swim class after swim class, beach trip after beach trip, visit after visit to my siblings' pools. He won't swim, and it doesn't seem to have anything to do with his being strong-willed (as we once thought) or not adventurous (as others have mentioned). My son is strong-willed, for sure, but he's never dug his heels in about anything quite the way he has about this. He is actually very adventurous in other ways. He loves to meet new friends, try different and exotic foods, and go to new summer camps; and he's quick to pick up a musical instrument or wade into the creek to catch crawfish. But he WILL NOT SWIM.

He's going to be six next week. We have plans to visit my brother again in California. We are going to a water park at the end of August. The kid must swim. So, last night, my husband started the nightly trips to the pool at the YMCA. My son sat on the steps of the pool for forty-five minutes. He wouldn't even get in the pool, telling my husband all the reasons why he didn't want to swim. But finally, he stepped down into the water. And finally, he kicked his feet and tried to swim.

When I was putting him to bed, he told me all about it. I could sense his disappointment that it took him so long to gain the courage to get into the pool. He told me that he was so scared of the water and that he was embarrassed that now, as an almost six-year-old, he couldn't swim. I explained to him all of the reasons why he needed to learn and that he just needed to do his best. That if he does his best, there is nothing to be embarrassed about. But if he won't even try, he will never know what he is capable of. As we snuggled in his bed, he grabbed me around the neck and whispered, "Well, I will just try harder tomorrow."

And really, isn't that all any one of us can do? We just need to try harder. As I lay with him, I thought back to the woman at the hospital all those years ago, trying hard to deliver a message to me—one that I did hear loud and clear: If we don't want to swim, no matter what the swimming entails, we don't need to swim. But if we don't try, how will we know that we don't want to? I'm hoping my son uses this as a lesson: Try new things. Be brave and courageous.

And if after you've tried, you decide you don't like it, that's fine. It's the effort that matters.

# TO THE GOOD MOTHER BUT BAD PARTNER

*L*

Motherhood means being superhuman at times. We perform the circus act that only a mother can handle of juggling multiple balls in the air. We run around the house doing our finest multitasking, at times with one baby on our back and one in our arms, while using our "free hand" to pick up the trail of toys that lay scattered in our path.

But when we are operating at full force, diving into complete *Mommy mode*, what about our partners? We have committed to each other; we are "works in progress" with a lifetime contract to help one another. But that takes patience, love, commitment, and tons of hard work. If it was easy, everyone would do it, and everyone's relationship would last. Frankly, and sadly, it's much easier to throw in the towel than to push through and do the hard work and daily maintenance that your partner and relationship require to thrive.

As a mother with three young children and another baby on the way, all who constantly need and rely on me, who require so much of my attention and patience and affection (not to mention the twenty young children I teach, coupled with the other balls I'm juggling in the air), what does that leave for my husband at the end of the day? This is something I struggle with on a daily basis. And if my marriage suffers, do my children suffer as well?

In case you weren't quite sure, the answer is *yes*.

If a couple who have children together think back to the time before they became parents, it comes as no surprise that life was very different. You held hands to and from the car. You finished each other's sentences because you were so in tune with one another's thoughts. You likely had in-depth conversations, no matter how long they needed to last.

You slept together, in more than one way, and on the weekends, you slept in for as long as you pleased. You left each other cute notes around the house, and throughout the workday you sent one another romantic texts and e-mails about how you couldn't wait to get home and see each other again.

Now there is constant chaos, tons of clutter, and unending noise. Instead of holding each other's hand, you're struggling to carry the diaper bag, hold a baby, and wipe another kid's nose, all while attempting to manage a cell phone, keys, and purse in the other hand, and hollering like a crazy person at another toddler who is trying to run away from you across the parking lot.

The cute notes have turned into e-mails and texts about how many diaper changes the baby has had and what your partner needs to grab at the grocery store on the way home. The long, thoughtful conversations that used to happen over dinner are now half sentences shouted over the babies and toddlers screaming and throwing their food, and finally, you officially give up and say, "I'll shoot you an e-mail or text to-morrow to tell you about it."

And the thought of having that alone time once the kids are in bed? Well, 9 times out of 10, I have already collapsed and passed out cold with one of the babies, because there wasn't one ounce of me able to stay awake a second longer.

It's inevitable; life changes after you bring a baby into the world *and* into your relationship. It changes *a lot*. So much the better, but with that also comes *different*, which can be straining on your relationship. But what happens when we devote all of our time and energy into being the best parent we can be, and our partner, naturally, and rightfully so, feels neglected?

Does that, in turn, at some point down the road affect your parenting individually and your coparenting as a team?

If you hadn't already guessed, the answer again is ab-solutely, without a doubt, **yes**.

But how do we *fix* this? Is there a quick fix? Unfortunately, I don't think there is. Trust me, after never-ending research and many disappointments, I have come to find that there isn't just a bandage to put over the seeping wounds that need to be loved and cared for. It takes a daily surrendering of one-self to be the partner you need to be.

Are the children fed? Are they changed? Are they warm and safe and sound? If all these areas of need are met, can you sneak five minutes of attention toward your partner to ask and truly listen about their day? Can you surprise them by going out of your way to wait on them, hand and foot, even if just for a few minutes, to make sure they have what they need and they are taken care of?

Some may wonder, *How does this even tie into making me a better mother?* How will my taking time from my children (and I know some of us don't have what seems to be an efficient amount of time already due to working), make my partner and me better parents? As far-fetched as this may seem, it's actually glaringly apparent: A better relationship between partners generates a better relationship with and *for* your children.

It's a proven fact that our children feed off of their environment. Our children feed off our moods, our words, and our actions, as well as our interactions. They look to us to see what love is, and hopefully we not only say it, but we show it. Actions speak alarmingly louder than words.

We've all heard the saying "A happy wife is a happy life." And I have to say, I agree completely, but, likewise, a happy marriage equals a happy family.

Sometimes it's not about how compatible we are through year after year and change after change, but rather how we deal with the incompatibility. It's safe to say that in any marriage over a week old, there are grounds for a divorce. The true test and trick is to find, and continue to seek out, grounds for *marriage*, for *love*, and for *supporting each other*.

The truth is, it's never equal. When one is giving 80 percent, the other might be giving only 20 percent. And yes, at times you will find yourself battling within your relationship as you feel like you're giving 100 percent while your partner isn't capable of giving anything.

As unfair as this is, we have to thank God for it. Thank God that one of you is able to hold on tight enough for you both.

Undoubtedly, a happy, thriving, healthy relationship between parents will manifest itself in happy, thriving, healthy children. Life is not perfect. Marriage is not perfect. Relationships are not perfect. Parenting is not perfect. But it's a matter of taking those imperfections, staring them straight in the face, and trying to make them a little *less* imperfect tomorrow.

Rome wasn't built in a day. All we can ask of our children, and of ourselves, is to take baby steps.

Meaningful, determined, sincere baby steps. And think of the difference we can potentially make over time.

Remember: Children are amazing imitators. Give them something, give them *someone*, to imitate.

# DEAR MOTHERS WHO RISE EARLY

*L*

The baby woke this morning very early, and it was as if she could hear the birds chirping over the rush of her humidifier, calling her to start the day. She pointed to the window, light starting to come through the blinds, and spoke her favorite hushed phrase of "What's that?" As sweet as she is, I simply wasn't ready to start the day. Smiling and giving her chubby cheek a kiss, I walked out of her darkened room, creeping past the opened door to my bedroom.

My son was sound asleep in our bed because he had come into our room in the middle of the night, relegating my husband to the sofa. We allow this to happen when he occasionally comes in because, as the days rush by, dawns like these turning to dusk, we know that soon he won't crawl in with us at all. On these nights, few and far between, I treasure his closeness and watch him sleep, being lulled to sleep myself by his presence.

Leaving him asleep in our bed, I took the baby downstairs to make a cup of coffee. My husband, an early riser, always leaves for work early, so it was just the two of us. My daughter continued to point to the window, excited by a new day. Prompted by her wonder for the dawn and the birds, I took her to the front porch to observe the world.

Morning had broken and it was beautiful. While I'm often awake late at night and in the middle of the night, I couldn't remember the last time I had witnessed this early of a morning, watching the earth spring to life outside. We took our spot on the front steps of our porch, and my daughter sat in my lap, gasping as each flower petal danced in the breeze. Her big, round blue eyes—the bluest eyes I've ever known—looked up at me in awe. Her strawberry blond hair glistened and came alive as the wind tousled her curls and the sun cast its perfect rays on her head. Her tiny mouth formed into a smile I'll always remember, her two little bottom teeth showing perfectly under the curl of her lip. Snug and secure in my lap, she continued to point at the birds and gasp at the bunny that seemed to come to see her at the base of the steps on which we were perched.

Sitting and holding her, with my firstborn asleep in bed, I saw the day through her eyes, the eyes of a baby seeing an early morning for the first time with all its intricacies—the dogwood petals blowing, the brown rabbit nibbling the grass, green and wet with dew. The world looked vibrant and alive. My baby girl was simply happy to be awake and in my arms, watching the morning as it unfolded before her eyes. Treasuring her, breathing in her hair and the smell of the last baby I will ever have, I gave thanks for the morning, for this child and the one still asleep. For the sun coming up over the tree line to shine on our garden. For the moon, retreating to allow the sun to make her way. For the rain, sure to come later in the day, nourishing all this new life.

My son's favorite prayer is a very simple one he said in preschool with his teachers. The prayer gives thanks for various simple things but mostly for the people in our lives. What a perfect sentiment and prayer to begin this day, this glorious early morning, holding a sweet baby who revels in seeing it all for the first time.

# TO THE GOOD MOM, THE BAD MOM, THE SUPERMOM

*L*

More than likely, your answer will vary depending upon the time you are asked this question. In most cases, we have a hard time answering anything above "a great mom" or "a superior mom," simply because of all the pressure we put on ourselves while we constantly compare our parenting to everyone else's.

There is a fine line for mothers when it comes to seeking out help, advice, and suggestions and then facing our own selves in the mirror, thinking, *Why didn't I think of that? I should have already tried that . . . months ago!* Or maybe even, *I already did that and, of course, it didn't work. Maybe it's just me?*

Sadly, we are living in an era of competitive parenting, where we find rivalry in the most contradictory areas. "*How many children do you have? Only two? Oh my, well I have four kids. You have no clue how busy and crazy my days are.*" And "*Does your baby sleep through the night? I don't believe in the cry-it-out method since that is just plain cruel, and I am up five to six times a night with mine. I just don't know how I even do it. You're so lucky you get to sleep.*" We almost find ourselves in the battle of whose children can rack up the most points by making our lives more tiring and difficult.

Trying to survive in this immodest society can do one of two things: It can motivate us and push us toward being the parents we need and want to become. But it can also motivate us to compare ourselves to others, which can be extremely detrimental and make us feel defeated and unworthy of the praise we actually deserve.

Because the truth is, we're all great mothers.

For those of us who put our needs at a distant second— wait, who are we kidding? A distant third, fourth, or fifth at times—at the end of the day, we really wouldn't have it any other way. If everyone else in the house is happy and has what they need, somehow that is more than sufficient for us.

A pat on the back goes both to mothers who bottle-feed their babies and to mothers who breast-feed their babies. Who are we to judge what works better for each mother and her baby? Are you nourishing your baby and feeding them when they need to be fed? GREAT. A gold star for you.

To the women who go off to work each day and have to leave their children behind or drop them off for childcare: This truly may be one of the hardest things you'll ever find yourselves doing. Kudos to us. Many days, I feel like we working moms should be called superheroes. Our heads spin with the hundreds of things we must accomplish in a single day's time and at the end of it, we ask ourselves, *Did I really just do all of that? TODAY?*

And to the stay-at-home mothers, the women who never leave their jobs, 24 hours a day, 7 days a week, I feel for you. For those who think this is a "cakewalk" deal for the mom, who's eating ice cream and watching cartoons all day with her feet propped up while her children are always smiling and happy and being great listeners...you are sadly mistaken. To be able to sneak away to the bathroom, by herself, without anyone pounding on the door...well, if she does happen to even make it inside alone, it would be nothing short of a miracle. The stay-at-home mothers, too, should be referred to as superheroes.

The mothers who use cloth diapers and the mothers who use disposables—props to you both! We all combat the same battles and conquer the same messes. And after some diaper changes, I feel like we should be awarded a big, beautiful medal. But to those of us who change our baby when needed, whether it be four times an hour or several times in the wee hours of the morning, we're doing what needs to be done, no matter what our choice or preference is for covering our baby's bottom.

Do you co-sleep with your baby? Do you let them cry it out? You've read three books on it and researched over ten articles on the pros and cons of both. Sometimes, when every person is telling us what is best for us and our baby, we forget to trust ourselves. Every family is different. Every child is different. A mother with multiple children will quickly tell you that what worked for one or two of her children did not work at all for another. We need to trust our gut instincts more often and do what works best for us and our kids. Sometimes we don't always want to listen to our gut, but it's almost always right.

To the mothers who get ridiculed for making time for them-selves or their partner (how selfish of them, right?)...Actually, *wrong*. I wish I were brave enough to make and take more "me" time and create more time for my husband and me—alone. It's so easy to get caught up in the daily chaotic race of just trying to make it from one drop-off to the next pickup, dashing off to the next event while your mind is spinning over the fifteen things on your list that need to be done once you get home—besides dinner, dishes, laundry, baths, and tuck-ins. Almost 9.9 times out of 10, though, you and your spouse are going to be better par-ents for having some alone time, and your children are going to see a stronger couple raising them. To those women who re-member "me time" and "partner time," you are not bad moms. You're essentially a wise mother who is trying to remember that all areas of your life, in fact, DO need attention—good for you!

What about those of us who are able to maintain perfectly organized, clean homes? And what about the ones who have a pile of toys in every spot in the house where they shouldn't be; not to mention the times you aren't quite sure what is stacked higher—the pile of dishes or laundry. Do these homes have "bad" mothers running them? No, certainly not. Those who are able to maintain it all flawlessly, and play with their children and give them the attention they need while meeting all of the day's demands—are doing an incredible job. I wish I fell into that category, but I do not. Although I can say this much: The days filled with chasing babies, legs aching from that many walks and wagon rides, sunburned cheeks from playing outside that long, and babies who whisper in your ear as you tuck them in, "This was the best day ever, Mommy!" Those are the days that I feel like I've truly accomplished something (a feeling of accomplishment that is better than what would follow any amount of housework being completed).

The truth of the matter is, the minute we stop comparing ourselves to the rest of the world and actually give ourselves a fighting chance, we will become open enough to see ourselves for who we really are as mothers. We need to evaluate ourselves fairly and weed out what's not working; give ourselves a fair amount of time to make needed changes and transitions; and, most importantly, encourage and remind one another of the incredible things we are accomplishing every single day.

The next time you are asked what kind of mother you are, smile, hold your head up high, and confidently say, "I am a supermom."

So...what kind of mother are you?

# TO THE MOM DROPPING HER CHILD OFF AT PRESCHOOL

*L*

I know how hard it is to drop a child off for preschool, to walk with tears in your eyes back to your car, feeling as if you've abandoned them. I know how hard it is to wait at home or work for hours, when you really just want to run to pick them up and hold them forever in your arms. So, Mama, let me help you through this. After all, we're all in this together and I want to help you as you, too, approach this milestone.

My daughter truly struggled with going to preschool. She's so fun-loving and friendly, so this was a surprise for us. The child I had always said was so independent suddenly cried when I left the room, clinging to me like a tiny koala bear. Her school is wonderful, her teacher is great, and she loves the other kids. I had no doubts in my mind about any of that, and she, herself, said the same thing. But she cried every morning for the first few weeks, her pale cheeks flushing to a bright red as tears spilled out of her blue eyes and onto her cheeks. Despite my best attempts to figure out what was going on, she simply said she missed me. She loved school but she missed home and me.

After about a minute she was fine until she saw her brother

at lunchtime in passing—he going in as she was leaving the lunchroom. And then the crying began again, and seeing him made her homesick, as he is the ever-constant reminder that she is not home with us all. She loves being at home and I love being at home, but after a wonderful summer, school is back in session.

I consulted my son's preschool teacher about this because he never cried when I left him. She's become a dear friend to me, as we bonded over the mothering of the boy we both loved. And her words really helped me to see the situation differently. She said she wonders if my daughter simply loves home so much that there's nowhere else she'd rather be. While that's kind of heartbreaking because she does need to spend time away from me, I loved the way she framed it. It helped me and so I thought it might help you, too?

So many kids don't have a home they miss while at school. I read all the time about kids who are neglected and abandoned. I've witnessed people being downright mean to their kids. I've heard horror stories of what home means to some children. Home isn't safe or fun, nurturing or reassuring.

And, all around me I hear stories of tears at drop-off. You might even have a toddler going through the same thing. Another child cried daily when I dropped my daughter off, too, at first. I, myself, never even went to preschool but was sad when I went to kindergarten and watched my brother walk away from me. I sat on my mom's lap until forever; her arms were my home and I simply loved being at home. I remember. I still love the home I've created with my own family more than any other single place. None of this is all that un-common despite what people might tell you.

And I guess, like my friend did for me, I'm here to help you reframe the tears at drop-off to daycare, preschool, school, college: Your children love home so much. They love home so much that some of them cry. Some of them miss you so much that they are brought to tears. And while that is so hard to reconcile, please remember how blessed you are to have created homes they love so very much. Truly. What an honor. And how lucky are our children, though some of them will cry because of it.

This is hard stuff even if people discount it. My letter to you is simply to give peace to parents with a heavy heart about the tears some kids shed. It's not at all easy to leave your heart behind. I wasn't sure I'd ever get used to it, even when my sweet girl did. But it did get easier and school be-came a home away from home for her.

While leaving them can be hard for us and for them, the security of home is what will give them the independence to spread their wings and fly, learning new things but always re-turning to the nest you've created safely for them.

# TO THE PRAYING MOTHER

*L*

What do we know about prayer?

Prayer heals.

Prayer manifests.

Prayer strengthens.

Prayer unifies.

Prayer conquers.

Prayer changes everything.

So the real question is, why don't we pray more often?

I have come to find that prayer and faith can be tremendously powerful, life-changing, and commanding, taking a supernatural form.

Faith can be defined as having complete trust and confidence in someone or something. It is safe to say that prayer and faith go hand in hand, and can be found in the deepest pocket of every Christian mother.

At the end of every single day, I can more easily count my mistakes than my successes as a mother. I lose my temper; my answer to a request is often *no* when it could have easily been *yes*; I take for granted the most special, perfect moments that are set before me and then forever gone.

However, the one thing that holds true for every day of my

life: I pray. And with that comes the beautiful waterfall effect of my children praying. Especially at such a young age, they are imitators and followers. They act as we do, not as we say. My children have already come to grow and trust and have such a genuine love for God that I feel at least I'm doing *something* right.

With our life and what we've been through and are currently undertaking and what is yet to come, the questions and comments aren't unexpected:

*"How are you going to manage this?"*

*"How will you get through that?"*

*"No one can handle all of that. It just doesn't seem possible."*

And so often my response is simply, "God's got this. He *has* it, so I *will* get through it, and I *will* do it."

I currently find myself at a crossroads. I will be giving birth to my fourth baby at the end of the summer. My *day* job is being an elementary teacher. I love it, I always have, and I always will. It truly may be one of the most rewarding professions on the planet.

However, one would think that time after time, baby after baby, passing each tiny one over to another's arms to be cared for would simply . . . get easier; that I would be used to it by now.

For those with that impression, let me gently correct you: You are *wrong*.

Hundreds of thousands of women do it. They have to do it. You must put in your time because you are one of the providers for this baby.

But it doesn't change the mind-boggling fact to me that I will soon have four small children, three of which will still be at *home*, including a newborn. The thought that at this point, under the given circumstances, I will once again hand over a tiny infant to another to care for is a gut-wrenching, horrifying, dreadful experience that I would not wish upon any living thing.

I can't tell you the number of battles I have had with my spouse over this. I can't tell you the number of battles I've had with *myself* over this. And I can't begin to tell you the number of self-loathing pity parties I have had over the thought of what is more than likely to come.

However, a couple of months ago I decided I was done. I was done fighting. I was done planning. I was done trying to figure out this master plan all on my own. For the first time in my entire life, I gave it all over completely to God.

Nothing is impossible for Him. And I realize that His plan for me and my heart's desires may not connect when I selfishly need or want that. But coming to the full realization that He has a better plan laid out before me...a plan better than I ever could imagine for myself with incessant prayer and overflowing trust, has satisfied me.

Do I think that relying on God's plan comes with a big fat check in the mail from an anonymous person that will help me pay off all my debt so I'll never have to work another day the rest of my life? Absolutely not.

Do I think that God's plan guarantees an easy, worry-free, tranquil path ahead of me? Absolutely not.

Do I think that every day will be full of smiles, and there will be no tears, no hardships, no problems if I turn my situation over to God? Absolutely not.

But I do think relying on God comes with grace. It comes with patience. It comes with understanding. It comes with trust. It comes with refinement. It comes with endurance. It comes with tolerance. It comes with strength. It comes with fortitude.

And most importantly, God's plan is a perfect plan. One that I may not understand for quite some time. My future will be an exact part of the master plan He has laid out for me—if I freely give myself and *my* own selfish plans and hopes over to God.

At the end of the day, I'm a stubborn, flawed, impatient, high-strung, overemotional woman. But thankfully I have One in this universe I can turn to who has the power to change my heart and ultimately guide my path toward becoming the person I am still meant to be.

When I'm lost, when I'm doubtful, when I'm worried, when I'm angry, when I'm anxious, when I'm frustrated, when I'm weak and tired and don't think I can make it through another day... *I pray.*

The power of a praying wife and mother... the power of prayer. Simply tell the doubters to step aside and watch it happen.

*Prayer.* It brings miracles.

# TO THE MOTHER WHO DOESN'T WEAR MAKEUP

*L*

"Mommy, why don't you wear makeup?"

My daughter asked me this today, and I wasn't too surprised, as I guess you could say I've been in a period of time where I'm doing "good" for the day if I've gotten my shower in and changed out of my workout clothes.

I've never been one to wear much makeup, and as a matter of fact, the makeup I do own is in a case that my mother got me when I was in high school; and some of the eye shadows in it are, well... it's safe to say *years* old.

As I watched my daughter carefully surveying my face, I had to wonder what was running through her mind. Maybe I looked different than I had a few weeks ago. It's sufficient to say I've earned the wrinkles that have accumulated on my face; and, likewise, the bags under my eyes have grown significantly since I started having babies nearly nine years ago.

I have three young daughters who study each and every one of my moves. And so I want them to be able to look in the mirror and not demean themselves or pick apart their imperfections, because it's in those imperfections that some of a woman's most unique beauty lies.

I want my daughters to take care of their skin and value their appearance, but I don't want them to compare themselves to others and feel that they need to look a certain way in imitation of someone else they hold in high esteem.

I want my daughters to grow into strong, independent, confident women who appreciate the natural beauty God has already blessed them with, a beauty that no makeup could ever enhance.

And likewise, I want my son to see women for their natural beauty, which comes from the inside out, and many times is hidden behind layers of unnecessary makeup.

I want my children to learn that beauty is determined in a number of ways.

You see, my children aren't going to remember that their mommy didn't have her face dolled up each day, or that she threw on nothing more than a little lip gloss in the way of makeup for church or a special event. My children aren't going to remember how much I aged through their childhood years; nor will they know how my growing wrinkles have bothered me more days than others. But I hope they remember that their mommy handled aging with grace and dignity and a bit of humor, and that she didn't take herself or her imperfections too seriously.

I want my children to look back and recall that their mommy taught them that beauty goes far deeper than what meets the eye.

I want them to remember the dance parties in the kitchen that were some of the most fun times they had, even if their mommy was in comfy clothes, with a messy bun on her head and no makeup on her face.

So I smiled and kissed my daughter's nose when she said again, "So, Mommy, why don't you?"

I looked her straight in the eyes and said, "Well, Mommy really didn't think I needed it today. What do you think?"

With that, my daughter smiled, wrapped her arms around my waist, and confidently replied, "Nope, you don't need it. I think you look pretty just the way you are."

# TO THE MOTHER WHO WANTS TO TEACH CARING

*L*

After a recent school field trip, my son said something to me, something so basic and yet so profound, that it got me to thinking that sometimes, all we need to do is show up in caring for the people in our lives.

My son took a field trip to a local farm with his kindergarten class, and because he's in a pre-K through eighth-grade school, the preschoolers went along with them. The school is good about teaching responsibility and fostering kindness, and so my son has a preschool buddy whom he is paired with on occasions such as these. A natural older brother, my son took his job with his preschool buddy quite seriously and told me all about it. Even though the trip was to a farm and they picked pumpkins, went on a hayride, and saw baby bunnies, when he told me about the trip, he mostly told me about his preschool buddy.

Because most kids are dropped off at his school, this was my son's first time on a school bus. And, I'm assuming it might have been the first time for his preschool buddy, too. He told me that because his little friend was younger and smaller, he put him by the window to ensure that he wouldn't fall out of the seat. He also held his hand the entire time. He explained that in the event of an accident, he was fully prepared to use his arm as a seat belt for his preschool buddy.

On the ride home from the farm, his preschool buddy fell asleep, and my son gave him his sweatshirt on which to rest his head. I told him I appreciated how nice he was to his preschool buddy. He looked at me and said, "Mama, I just took care of him because he needed me." He said it matter-of-factly, like caring for our friends is the most basic thing in the world.

He showed up for his preschool buddy and he took care of him because he simply needed to. He did it without question or consideration for how he, himself, might feel to be sitting by the aisle without a seat belt, because he knew his preschool buddy might find it a bit more daunting.

All too often, we look inward instead of at the people around us; I think we are all guilty of this from time to time. But if we look at the faces of the people around us, we just might see someone who needs us, maybe even more than we need them. How many problems could be avoided or solved if we just showed up and cared for one another, without question, without expectation?

In the often self-absorbed world we live in, taking care of people can be a blessing, not only to them but to us. My son reminded me of this with his simple statement and the pride in his voice. He felt rewarded for taking care of his friend. He reminded me that we're all in this together, and generosity of spirit really is our utmost gift back to the world.

This week, I received an e-mail from a very busy friend because she sensed that my week had started off a little rocky. She juggles much more than I do, but she took the time to check in on me. It took her less than two minutes to type the e-mail, and ultimately, I didn't require anything of her, but her very simple message meant the world to me. I'm lucky to have people in my life who show they care when I need them, even though their lives are as full as mine. And, in return, I try to show up for them. Maybe we miss the mark from time to time, but we do try to show one another that we care.

We all feel bogged down at times with our own trials, fears, or insecurities. But being available for someone else might just be the push we need to gain perspective on the beauty in our lives. It doesn't take very long to send a text to check in on a friend and say you care. It takes just a minute to cut a few flowers from the garden, stick them in a mason jar, and walk around the corner to deliver them to a neighbor who just might need a pick-me-up. Simple, caring gestures to say, *I'm here for you because you need me. You are my people.*

The field trip to the farm provided my son with a lesson it seems he already knew: We care for people when they need us. We call them our people. We give them our sweatshirts or protect them with our arms. And I'm thankful that he reminded me of this. After all, we're all in this together.

# THIS IS THE LETTER FOR EVERY MOTHER

*L*

*This* is the letter for every mother.

We are every mother, holding hands here on the page, united by our experiences.

We are mothers, working late into the night, trying to make our dreams come true so our children will be brave enough to try, too.

We are mothers, showing our kids what passion is and what hard work looks like.

We are mothers, learning and leading, learning and leading.

We are mothers, keeping our arms wide open and remembering that our arms are home for our children.

We are mothers, guiding our children through life, no matter where they are, young or old, near or far.

We are mothers of sons, and we try hard to show them they're brave, even if they cry (and *because* they cry), and that being kind is more important than anything else.

We are mothers of daughters, and we want them to know they are strong—in all ways—and on days when they don't feel so strong, there will be other women to lift them up.

We are mothers, showing our children what love is and how it will follow them, always.

We are mothers, doing our best to keep our feet planted firmly on the ground.

We are mothers, doing the ordinary: feeding our families, tending our homes.

We are mothers, listening, loving, playing, nurturing.

We are mothers, saying we're sorry and trying, trying, trying harder every day to do better.

We are mothers, learning how to let go and be still.

We are mothers, surrounding ourselves with people who love us and saying good-bye to those who don't.

We are mothers, keeping our people close.

We are mothers, bowing our heads in prayer and keeping our hands open.

We are mothers, seeing the extraordinary in the ordinary, the beauty in the mundane.

We are mothers, in a community of many mothers, here on the page.

We are mothers, in a tribe of mothers, made stronger by one another.

We are every mother, holding hands here on the page.

This is the letter for every mother.

*L*

When my son lost his first tooth last fall, it fell from his mouth, blood dripping into his hand, and he laughed. The grass was still very green, but the leaves beyond his head, in their brilliant shades of persimmon and gold, seemed to tell the story: The fall season was upon us, and with the leaves that would soon fall from the trees, my son's baby teeth were beginning to fall out, one by one. And just like the winter that inevitably followed that fall and every one since, his baby teeth did fall out.

That day I said good-bye to a stage of my baby boy's life, but in the change, there is beauty. In the change, there is an awakening. All we need to do is look closely.

With that first tooth, my son looked in the mirror many times a day and wiggled it. We inspected it before he went to school each day, and as soon as we got home, he yelled for me to come see how loose his tooth had become. The tooth hung on, however, and even as his pap offered to pull it for him, the tooth remained.

After school one day in the grass beside his classroom, he played a game of catch with his best friend. The tooth came out when the boys bumped into one another. When it finally fell from his mouth, his face told the story: He was in shock but so very happy. The blood dripped from his mouth in all its gory glory and surprised him. At first, I thought he would cry, but instead, his face bloomed into the smile I'll always know, suddenly changed because he had finally lost his first tooth.

A permanent tooth quickly replaced the spot where the baby tooth once had been and many have fallen from his mouth since that fall day over a year ago. In actions that seemingly took forever, the teeth broke free and so many adult teeth now fill his smile. When I look at him now, I can see his adult smile—the one I'll look at forever—and just like that, my baby boy has become a big boy. Even though that change has come in various phases, I always remember how the first tooth made me realize that while he had baby teeth (and still has a few left), he truly isn't a baby anymore.

Now his pants are always too short—the ones I just bought at the beginning of the school year need to be replaced. His neck is thinner and while his rounded cheeks are still there (*they are, aren't they?*), his face is taking the shape of the teenager he'll one day become. His eyes, once very blue and then gray, have changed. They have the slightest hint of amber in them—just right around the pupil. I see my son every day, but the changes always surprise me, as they seemingly happen overnight.

The experience of my son and the loss of teeth caused me to pay closer attention to my daughter's tiny mouth and perfect teeth. She now has a full set of teeth, fifteen the last time I checked, and some molars are currently breaking through.

How can my baby have fifteen teeth? But even as I type the word "baby," she's not at all one. While she's the baby of our family, she's actually a toddler, running and playing, talking in complete sentences. Just this week, she wrote an "M" for her name. And the cycle of life is so surreal sometimes: She is finally getting some of her last baby teeth as my son is losing his last ones. I have learned that there is nothing as constant as change.

Teeth have fallen out and luckily, I have been there with a tissue when they do, to wipe the blood from the smiling face of the child I'm just so lucky to have. And while we sometimes mourn the passing of time, in the end, we simply need to watch as the gifts are revealed in these ever-present changes.

# I'M *JUST* A MOM

*L*

I'm *just* a mom who no longer knows what to tell her children when they ask why there is so much pain and hurt and so many "bad guys" in this world.

I'm *just* a mom who continually questions herself every day, second-guessing every decision and rethinking every move she's made.

I'm *just* a mom who is no stranger to hard work, pure exhaustion, and recurring disappointments... despite her best efforts.

I'm *just* a mom who is trying to instill confidence and a sense of self-worth in her daughters and a drive of sheer determination and respect in her son; reminding all four of her children to be fearless in their dreams.

I'm *just* a mom who is continuing to fight what some think is an unrealistic battle, a battle for every working parent in our country to have a fighting chance to experience the most important thing in this world with their newborn: time.

I'm *just* a mom who still struggles trying to tell her children to always look for the good in the world, despite the horrific tragedies that we hear of every day. Because wherever there is tragedy, we can always find the "good guys" close by.

I'm *just* a mom who continues to make mistakes each day, who breaks down in tears, who has trouble forgiving herself for what she failed to do or what she could have done better.

I'm *just* a mom who is crazy enough to believe she can change the world if she is persistent, knowing she has the most powerful One on her side.

I'm *just* a mom who has worked several jobs at once, yet still has come up short, having to scrape change out of her children's piggy banks for groceries and worrying how she will pay the next overdue bill.

I'm *just* a mom who has had to fake it more days than not, because there is nothing at all to be gained by her children sensing her fear.

I'm *just* a mom who wants to be seen as a hero in the eyes of four tiny humans who are constantly watching, constantly learning, and constantly studying each and every move she makes.

I'm *just* a mom who is no better than anyone else; a flawed woman who is her own worst critic, yet is trying to learn to love and accept herself a little more each day.

I'm *just* a mom who lives in a time when her heart will sink each time she kisses her children good-bye as they leave for school, for so many reasons, some of which should never have to cross her mind.

I'm *just* a mom who has taken some big risks in order to produce some big rewards and who puts her head down and works tirelessly, as giving up isn't an option.

However, I'm one of the lucky ones.

Because I'm *that* mom who felt convicted to continue on, to push past and go up against what was considered the norm.

I'm *that* mom who has learned one of the toughest lessons of parenthood and decided to finally stop caring about what others think and care more about what her gut tells her to do.

I'm *that* mom who has let her faith be much bigger than her fear.

I'm *that* mom who is still a work in progress, but with God's help, is trying to use each and every mistake to better herself not only as a wife and a mother...but as an individual.

Yes, I'm *that* mom who has given herself no choice but to fail her way to success; going a little further even when her fuel tank is empty.

And I'm *that* mom who will continue to fight tooth and nail for this world to be a better place for her children and grand-children.

I'm *just* a mom who believes one day we'll get to say, "We believed we could...and we did."

# TONIGHT, WE WISH FOR YOU

*L*

Tonight, we wish for you, our sweet friends, to be renewed by our letters.

Tonight, we wish for you to hold our hands on the page despite time or distance, race, creed, or color.

Tonight, we are all friends. Here, hold our hands.

Tonight, we are mothers, friends, sisters, aunts, grandmothers, nieces, cousins.

Tonight, we are single, married, or divorced. But love lives in our hearts, no matter what.

Tonight, we are from all over the world, but we unite on these pages, friends in motherhood.

Tonight, we will make dinner and do laundry. We will read stories, draw baths, and tuck children into bed. But even as they sleep, all we'll think about is them.

Tonight, we are young or we are old. We are all at different stages, but we are mothers, all the same.

Tonight, we might get overwhelmed and lose our cool, but we will apologize and try again tomorrow.

Tonight, we are moms of children of all ages who are home with us or who have left our nest, but no matter what, we will always be their mother.

Tonight, we wish for you a friend who picks you up when you're down.

Tonight, we wish for you a friend who invites you over for tea in your pajamas.

Tonight, we wish for you a friend who sees you for who you really are—right beyond the superficial trappings of life. This friend doesn't care what car you drive or don't drive; she doesn't care if you wear current styles or if you're still wearing a sweatshirt from 1993.

Tonight, we wish for you a tribe of soul sisters—women who show up without fail to hold your hand.

Tonight, we wish for you a friend who invites you to come with her to Target because she knows you love it there and it will brighten your mood. And even though you buy only shampoo and toothpaste, pencils and snacks for lunches, you still laugh and walk together through the store.

Tonight, we wish for you friends who take the time to see how you're doing because they actually care about you. They reach out to you. That is no small thing.

Tonight, we wish for you a friend who loves your children and helps you in whatever stage you're in.

Tonight, we wish for you to be held in the palm of God's hand.

Tonight, we wish joy for you and we thank you for being here with us.

Tonight, you are every mother and our dear friends.

# Acknowledgments

*Kara would like to acknowledge and thank the following:*

God, for the gift of being a mother. It all begins and ends for me there.

My sweet children, Matt and Maggie. I love you more than words can say. Without you, I wouldn't be who I am. You are simply all I ever dreamed of and prayed for. Thank you for showing me the way—the light, the path—when I was lost.

My husband, Mike, for being my best friend and the tree that keeps me tethered. Thank you for spending this life with me and encouraging me always to reach for the sun by climbing on your branches.

My parents, Ray and Donna, for showing me well that parenting never ends. Thank you for loving me like you do and for showing up, without fail, when I need you.

My siblings, Kelly and Ray, for walking beside me through life and loving my children like your own.

Regan, for reminding me to answer God's call, which came in the form of her asking me to collaborate on what became this book. She truly walks like a disciple and has helped me grow in so many ways. I'm honored to write alongside her in *A Letter for Every Mother* and to call her my dear friend.

Our editor, Keren Baltzer, and our agent, Rachel Ekstrom, and everyone at Center Street, for believing in our words and this project. To Arianna Huffington, Jill Smokler, and Tori Grenz for the beautiful endorsements for this project and to Ashley Willis for writing the perfect foreword.

To all the women I mother with: the Blessed Mother, my Meemom, Mom, sister, sisters-in-law, mother-in-law, aunts, cousins, my day-to-day mom tribe, and my faraway kindred spirit friends, my children's teachers, and my readers on *Mothering the Divide*, this is for you. You are every mother. You have lifted me up, reminded me of what matters, held me, hugged me, prayed for me, given me cups of coffee and glasses of wine. Thank you for mothering the divide with me here and now and forever. I am so grateful.

*Regan would like to acknowledge and thank the following:*

I feel like this book was so divinely orchestrated to be written from the very start. As long of a journey as it seems to have been, God truly laid the pieces out so perfectly for this project to fall into place.

I could not have hand picked a better co-author, and I am eternally grateful Kara said yes when I approached her with this idea. Her writing style is so poignant and so touching, I knew that millions needed to read her words and be as moved by them as I was.

Our agent, Rachel Eckstrom, our editor, Keren Baltzer,

and our publisher, Center Street, have played the most integral part in making this dream come to fruition. They have made this project seem effortless and have taken as much pride and genuine enthusiasm in bringing it to completion as we have.

I will forever be grateful to Jill Smokler and Arianna Huffington who both shared my writing on their phenomenal platforms; it truly laid the steps in order for me to continue to grow on this journey.

So often I have been asked how I come up with my material and find the way to speak to so many through my writing, and I can only respond with the same three brutally honest words, "I live it."

My four children Kendyl, Kaden, Kennedy, and Kelsey leave me with more than enough inspiration on a daily basis to tell "our story" countless families can relate to.

Terry, my one and only, we have made it through the impossible—forever, for always and no matter what. To think of how far we've come...

This beautiful mess, the rewarding exhaustion, and the thrilling roller coaster that I get to ride daily, well...I wouldn't trade it for anything else in this entire world.

I'm humbled to share this imperfectly perfect life my husband and I have created together, that we simply try to survive one day at a time.

Thank you to our readers for sharing in our journey to speak and relate to every mother through our experiences and where we have been blessed to have found true inspiration.

# About the Authors

**Kara Lawler** has been married to her high school sweetheart for sixteen years, is the mother of two small children who inform all of her writing and her perspective, and has been an English teacher for sixteen years. Together with her family, she does small-scale farming on the family homestead in the Allegheny Mountains of Pennsylvania. Kara's work has been featured on the *Huffington Post*, the *Today Show*, *Parenting.com*, *Scary Mommy*, and *Mamalode*, among other places. Her work has also been reviewed online on *Reader's Digest*, *MSN*, and other media outlets. You can find Kara on her blog, *Mothering the Divide* (motheringthedivide.com), where she writes about the divide that is mothering children while still mothering her own spirit and the sacred.

**Regan Long** has been married for over ten years and has four young children. She was able to retire from teaching at thirty-one, due to being an entrepreneur with her home business and now helps hundreds of other mothers around the United States, Canada, and the UK to be able to build businesses from home. Regan is also a paid family leave advocate and has developed her own online parenting course, *Rainbow Reactions Parenting*. She is the founder of *The Real Deal of Parenting*, REGANLONG.COM and is an influencer for Mogul, an award-winning platform for women that reaches 18 million women per week. She's worked with award-winning film director Ky Dickens on the first-ever film on the subject of paid family leave and works with influential members of government and nonprofits on family leave issues. Regan writes regularly for *Today Parents*, *HuffPost Parents*, *Parenting.com*, *Mamalode*, and *Scary Mommy*.